access to history *in depth*

CHARTISM

Harry Browne

Hodder & Stoughton

A MEMBER OF THE HODDER HEADLINE GROUP

Acknowledgments

The publishers would like to thank the following for permission to use copyright illustrations: Mary Evans Picture Library, p. 32; The British Library Picture Library, p. 39; The National Museum of Labour History, p. 95; The Illustrated London News Picture Library, p. 96.

The publishers would like to thank the following for permission to reproduce material in the volume: Cambridge University Press for an extract from *London Chartism 1838-1848* by David Goodway (1982) and extracts from *1848. The British State and the Chartist Movement* by John Saville (1987); Frank Cass for extracts from *History of the Chartist Movement 1837-1854*, 2nd edition by R.G. Gammage (1969); Croom Helm for extracts from *The Lion of Freedom* by James Epstein (1982); George Allen and Unwin for extracts from *Bronterre* by A. Plumer (1971); Heinemann for extracts from *The Chartist Challenge: A Portrait of George Julian Harney* by A.R. Schoyen (1958); Lawrence and Wishart for an extract from *Ernest Jones: Chartist* by John Saville (1952); Longman for an extract from *Chartism, 3rd edition* by Edward Royle (1996); Macmillan for extracts from *'Trade Unionism' in Popular Movements* by W.H. Fraser, (ed.) J.T. Ward (1970) and the 'The Language of Chartism' by Gareth Steadman Jones and 'Some Organisational and Cultural Aspect of the Chartist Movement in Nottingham' by James Epstein in *The Chartist Experience: Studies in Working-Class Radicalism and Culture 1830-60*, (ed.) James Epstein and Dorothy Thompson (1952); Manchester University Press for extracts from *The Chartist Movement* by Mark Hovell (1918); McGibbon and Kee for an extract from *Life and Struggles* by William Lovett (1967); Temple Smith for extracts from *The Chartists* by Dorothy Thompson (1984); Unwin for extracts from *The Anti-Corn Law League* by Norman McCord (1968).

Every effort has been made to trace and acknowledge ownership of copyright. The publishers will be glad to make suitable arrangements with any copyright holders whom it has not been possible to contact.

I should like to record a particular word of thanks to my General Editor, Dr R.D. Pearce, and to Keith Crook. Dr Pearce, by his perceptive criticsm and advice, helped to shape the book's final form. Keith Crook gave generously of his time not only in reading the book in its various stages but also in drawing the computerised diagrams.

British Library Cataloguing in Publication Data
A catalogue for this title is available from the British Library

ISBN 0 340 72070 0

First published 1999

Impression number	10	9	8	7	6	5	4	3	2
Year		2004	2003	2002	2001				

Cover picture shows the Chartists taking their petition to Parliament in 1843, reproduced courtesy of Weidenfeld and Nicolson Archives.

Typeset by Sempringham publishing services, Bedford
Printed in Great Britain for Hodder & Stoughton Educational,
a division of Hodder Headline Plc, 338 Euston Road, London NW1 3BH
by The Bath Press, Bath

Contents

Preface

The original *Access to History* series was conceived as a collection of sets of books covering popular chronological periods in British history, such as 'the Tudors' and 'the nineteenth century', together with the histories of other countries, such as France, Germany, Russia and the USA. This arrangement complemented the way in which early-modern and modern history has traditionally been taught in sixth forms, colleges and universities. In recent years, however, other ways of dividing up the past have become increasingly popular. In particular, there has been a greater emphasis on studying relatively brief periods in considerable detail and on comparing similar historical phenomena in different countries. These developments have generated a demand for appropriate learning materials, and, in response, two new 'strands' are being added to the main series - *In Depth* and *Themes*. The new volumes build directly on the features that have made *Access to History* so popular.

To the general reader

Although *Access* books have been specifically designed to meet the needs of examination students, these volumes also have much to offer the general reader. *Access* authors are committed to the belief that good history must not only be accurate, up-to-date and scholarly, but also clearly and attractively written. The main body of the text (excluding the 'Study Guides') should, therefore, form a readable and engaging survey of a topic. Moreover, each author has aimed not merely to provide as clear an explanation as possible of what happened in the past but also to stimulate readers and to challenge them into thinking for themselves about the past and its significance. Thus, although no prior knowledge is expected from the reader, he or she is treated as an intelligent and thinking person throughout. The author tends to share ideas and explore possibilities, instead of delivering so-called 'historical truths' from on high.

To the student reader

It is intended that *Access* books should be used by students studying history at a higher level. Its volumes are all designed to be working texts, which should be reasonably clear on a first reading but which will benefit from re-reading and close study. To be an effective and successful student, you need to budget your time wisely. Hence you should think carefully about how important the material in a particular book is for you. If you simply need to acquire a general grasp of a topic, the following approach will probably be effective:

1. Read Chapter 1, which should give you an overview of the whole book, and think about its contents.

2. Skim through Chapter 2, paying particular attention to the opening section and to the headings and sub-headings. Decide if you need to read the whole chapter.
3. If you do, read the chapter, stopping at the end of every sub-division of the text to make notes.
4. Repeat stage 2 (and stage 3 where appropriate) for the other chapters.

If, however, your course - and your particular approach to it - demands a detailed knowledge of the contents of the book, you will need to be correspondingly more thorough. There is no perfect way of studying, and it is particularly worthwhile experimenting with different styles of note-making to find the one that best suits you. Nevertheless, the following plan of action is worth trying:

1. Read a whole chapter quickly, preferably at one sitting. Avoid the temptation - which may be very great - to make notes at this stage.
2. Study the flow diagram at the end of the chapter, ensuring that you understand the general 'shape' of what you have read.
3. Re-read the chapter more slowly, this time taking notes. You may well be amazed at how much more intelligible and straightforward the material seems on a second reading - and your notes will be correspondingly more useful to you when you have to write an essay or revise for an exam. In the long run, reading a chapter twice can, in fact, often save time. Be sure to make your notes in a clear, orderly fashion, and spread them out so that, if necessary, you can later add extra information.
4. Read the advice on essay questions, and do tackle the specimen titles. (Remember that if learning is to be effective, it must be active. No one - alas - has yet devised any substitute for real effort. It is up to you to make up your own mind on the key issues in any topic.)
5. Attempt the source-based questions. The guidance on tackling these exercises, which is generally given at least once in a book, is well worth reading and thinking about.

When you have finished the main chapters, go through the 'Further Reading' section. Remember that no single book can ever do more than introduce a topic, and it is to be hoped that - time permitting - you will want to read more widely. If *Access* books help you to discover just how diverse and fascinating the human past can be, the series will have succeeded in its aim - and you will experience that enthusiasm for the subject which, along with efficient learning, is the hallmark of all the best students.

Robert Pearce

1 Introduction

'As soon as the House of Commons incorporates the will, not of the bourgeoisie alone, but of the whole nation, it will absorb the whole power so completely, that the last halo must fall from the head of the monarch and the aristocracy'.[1] So declared the German socialist Friedrich Engels in 1845 from the vantage point of Manchester, that symbol of a new society bursting at the seams which industrialisation was creating. This still remains an unfulfilled prophecy for although the aristocracy may have been replaced by the new icons of footballers, television 'personalities' and columnists, the halo around the monarch, although dimmer, is still visible. However, this vision of the future so appealing to Engels, a Chartist sympathiser, was viewed with horror by the opponents of Chartism who saw the end of civilisation as they knew it in the enfranchisement of the unpropertied mass of the nation. On the one hand, hope of improvement and, on the other, fear of social disaster. This conflict which divided much of Britain in the years from 1838 to 1848 had nothing in common with the shadow boxing of modern politics but was an issue which on both sides aroused deep feelings, often of great hostility to those who were on the other side of the class divide represented by the ownership of property.

The very name 'Chartist' conjured up for many of the middle class a stereotype of the unshaven, illiterate, working man, shifty and loud-mouthed and often the worse for too many hours spent in beerhouses or taverns. This made it difficult for them to see the reality of the Chartist sympathiser, who was often literate, sometimes a Temperance man, and normally essentially law-abiding.

Chartists met together in the little free time left after an exhausting working week, spent hours studying the Chartist press, gave their pennies to fund the movement and strove zealously to win hearts and minds to their cause. Without exaggeration, they can be compared to converts to such a religious movement as early Methodism in their willingness to sacrifice time and energy to bring nearer that day when the Charter would become law. There was, they believed, a new world waiting be be born when their just demands had finally been met.

What perhaps is most remarkable about Chartism is that it existed at all. It is too facile to see it as no more than the sum of all the discontents of the time - the New Poor Law, the unregulated factory hours amongst the most significant - for the fundamental driving force was something quite different: a demand for political equality as expressed in the franchise. Chartists were convinced that, armed with the power that the vote would give them, other grievances could readily be dealt with. On this rock, they built a movement in which the Victorian concept of self-help was enshrined. It is of great historical importance, for not only was Chartism the first organised labour movement in Britain, but by reason of Britain's lead in that process of industrialising which was to transform Europe - and then the rest of the world - it was also the first movement of its kind in the world.

1 Forerunners

Most historical movements build on the legacy of the past, and in this respect Chartism was no exception. Eighteenth-century ideas of the Rights of Man, proclaimed so vigorously during the French Revolution, were embedded in Chartism, together with assertions on the nature of political justice inherited from Tom Paine. Some of the traditional tactics of earlier popular movements could be seen in crowd behaviour in provincial cities such as Bradford where at times Chartists seized control of the town. Yet many other characteristics, such as the practice of convening Chartist Parliaments, were peculiar to the movement itself.

In the 20-odd years before the emergence of Chartism, there had been other working-class political movements, some like the Hampden Clubs, which were relatively short-lived. These sprang into life in 1816 with a call for universal suffrage and were particularly vigorous in the northern manufacturing districts. Others such as the co-operatives and comprehensive trade unionism arose mainly from the fertile mind of the socialist manufacturer Robert Owen. Again, it was Owen himself who revived interest in the idea of agrarian communities based on brotherhood and equality of provision. These diverse responses to social change might be seen as an alternative way forward to that chosen by the Chartists - and one which was to provide models in the years after the collapse of the movement.

Chartism's inheritance from the past was also intellectual and ideological. From William Cobbett, the most famous journalist of his day, a self-taught countryman, they took the conviction that the only way of tackling the corruption which was at the heart of the political system was to give to all a share in political power - and that the way of achieving that was by making their message heard throughout the land. For Cobbett, the means was the press, through his *Political Register*, and the Chartists were to follow this tradition with their own journal, the *Northern Star*, and to build on it by using the Methodist tactic of sending out lecturers as missionaries to hammer home their message. From Tom Paine's *Rights of Man*, they drew a searing analysis of the blight of inherited privilege and wealth and the certainty that the cure lay in universal suffrage. Although occasional lip service was paid to the need to make this demand truly universal, nevertheless the Chartist call for 'universal suffrage' usually meant 'universal male suffrage'.

2 The Chartist Movement: An Overview

Chartism arose from the many diverse campaigns of the 1830s, some concerned to right the new wrongs such as the 1834 Poor Law

Amendment Act that the Whig government were seen to have imposed on the working class, others to bring much-needed improvement to their lives. Its birth-date is usually give as 6 August 1838, for on that day the leaders of the movement expounded the Charter with its Six Points to a mass meeting in Birmingham. The Charter itself had been drawn up in the preceding year by a new body, the London Working Men's Association, and had been published in May 1838. It proposed far-reaching constitutional changes, the famous Six Points. If the Charter became law, there would be universal male suffrage, no property qualifications for MPs, annual Parliaments, equal electoral districts, payment of MPs and a secret ballot. In the history of the movement, one other event was also crucial: the first publication of the *Northern Star* on 18 November 1837.

During the winter of 1838/9, the movement gathered pace, with crowded meetings in the North and in Scotland and with Feargus O'Connor, the Irish barrister, emerging as its much-loved leader. The meetings in turn amassed signatures to a Petition to be presented to Parliament calling for the Charter to become the law of the land. On 4 February 1839, the first Chartist Convention met in London to plan its strategy. The Petition was presented to a largely unsympathetic House of Commons on 14 June and the Convention then moved to Birmingham to consider the next move, the 'ulterior measures' to force the government's hand such as a general strike. After riots in the Bull Ring, the town centre, several Chartists were arrested. Against this background, the House of Commons rejected the Chartist Petition on 12 July by 235 votes to 46.

The year ended with the tragic events in Newport, South Wales when an ill-conceived march of miners and ironworkers on the town led to the death of 24 Chartists and to a wave of arrests, in all 125, of whom 21 were charged with the capital offence of high treason. In the event, none were executed but the leaders were sentenced to transportation for life.

By the end of that year, most of the main leaders were either in prison or awaiting trial and more than 500 of the rank and file were sentenced to varying terms of imprisonment.

In 1840, Chartism re-grouped and on 20 July the National Charter Association was founded which, through its elected executive, was to act as guide and convener to the movement, empowered to call a Convention, the Chartist alternative Parliament, as and when necessary. By the end of 1841, a new Petition was being planned for submission in the following year. That year, 1842, was critical for Chartism. Not only was a Petition with more than 3 million signatures presented to Parliament (where it was rejected) but a rival body, the Complete Suffrage Union, founded in Birmingham by a Quaker merchant, Joseph Sturge, tried - and failed - to take control of the reform movement. Frustrated in his attempts to secure the franchise for working men, Feargus O'Connor turned aside from direct political action and proposed an ambitious scheme, the Land Plan, to re-settle town workers in agricultural communities, a move which antagonised some long-term supporters.

During the middle years of the 1840s, a time of relative economic stability, the movement was quiescent, but was quickened into life again by the downturn in the economy in the winter of 1847-8. The new phase began with the election of O'Connor in July as MP for Nottingham and was followed by the now familiar round of meetings and the collection of signatures. It ended on 10 April 1848 when the third Petition was delivered to Parliament, with London in a state of siege. Its failure - and the public humiliation which followed the revelation that many of the signatures were bogus - sent Chartism into terminal decline. There was, however, an aborted rising in London on 15 August, followed by another series of arrests and trials.

Although the Chartist movement remained active for another ten years, it never regained its earlier strength and popular support. O'Connor withdrew and a new leader, Ernest Jones, took over control of the rump of the movement. In 1851, a NCA Convention accepted a broadly socialist policy, making history as the first British working-class social democratic party. By now, the drive for large-scale political change had long since gone and in 1858, with its leaders' acceptance of a pact with middle-class radicals pledged to work for limited reform, the movement came to an end.

During its short yet dramatic history, Chartism stayed as it began - in general, well within the confines of the law. It started as a major pressure group, using the historic remedy of the petition to Parliament to secure justice, and then, in the Convention, created a short-lived alternative to Parliament itself. And with the single perplexing exception of the Newport Rising, it remained almost entirely non-violent. There was indeed much talk of 'ulterior measures' but these generally never went beyond ill-conceived plans for a general strike. Nevertheless, both in 1840 and in 1848 there is evidence of plans for an armed rising. In some towns such as Bradford, a particularly turbulent centre, Chartists were armed, usually with pikes made by the local blacksmith, but to arm in self-defence was within their constitutional rights. They insisted their purpose was entirely defensive and a safeguard against a surprise attack by the forces of the state. Property was sometimes threatened and, on occasion, the houses of unpopular local gentry were ransacked. Yet there were no organised attacks upon the person. Given the contemporary middle-class fear of that many-headed beast, the 'mob', this record was a remarkable tribute to the self-discipline of a movement comprising many thousands of men and women who at times were at starvation point.

3 The Historical Debate

The way in which Chartism has been studied by historians and their appreciation of its importance has undergone significant changes in recent years. Initially, under the influence of its first historian, Mark Hovell, its working-class supporters were seen as a misguided mob awaiting an opportunity to overturn a well-balanced and civilised society. At their head was a wild and incoherent Irishman, given to fierce invective and prone to lead his unthinking followers into blind alleys - or at worst, into hopeless conflict against the established order. This interpretation has been gradually replaced by an appreciation of the range of ability and the diverse skills of the movement's many leaders. Recent historians, too, have emphasised the quality of Feargus O'Connor's leadership as well as his commitment to the cause. Like politicians in other times, Chartists were sensitive to changing currents of thought and, as a consequence, some of its leaders were anxious to tie Chartism in with such new directions as the Temperance Movement or the Evangelical Revival. Such offshoots which then appeared, like Temperance Chartism or Christian Chartism, still stayed within the broad church of the movement. A founder member, William Lovett, was to turn to education for the working class as offering a long-term solution, and another leader, Bronterre O'Brien, to socialism. What they all had in common was a continuing commitment to making the Charter the law of the land.

Chartists have been readily divided into 'moral force' and ' physical force' men, almost as if there were two entirely distinct groups, each trying to push or pull the movement in one direction or the other. In this categorisation, the 'physical force' men were prepared to use force or that threat of force which had seemed to 'persuade' the government in 1832 to pass the Reform Act. 'Moral force' men were those who believed in the power of rational argument and reckoned that in the end the reasonableness of their demands would win over public opinion. Yet the reality was quite different in that there was a wide spectrum of opinion on the question of when, if at all, the use of force was legitimate. If the model of the state used by the Chartists was that of an unjust power exercised over a submissive people (as their rhetoric seemed to suggest), then there was sound historical precedent to justify an uprising against a tyrant. Some Chartist leaders, notably the young Julian Harney, went far beyond that and advocated a popular revolution, with the example of the French Revolutions of 1789 and 1830 very much in mind. However, revolutionary activity, whatever its theoretical basis, shaded over in the minds of many Chartists into a justification of the use of force if attacked. The great debate on force as the ultimate sanction took place mainly in the 1839 Convention and frightened off many moderate-minded delegates. But in considering this issue, one question should be asked: what hope of success did either policy have? Doesn't this question of the 'failure' of Chartism to which the physical force versus moral force debate, as well as the quality of leadership, in part all relate, turn on 'that assumption of the possibility of success' so often made ?[2] Given the nature of English society and government', were not, as Asa Briggs suggests, 'the cards too heavily stacked against them'?[3]

How far, if at all, was Chartism no more than a response to distress, and to the sometimes sudden contractions of the new market economy? Certainly a study of its peak periods in 1839, 1842, and 1848 suggests that economic distress quickened the pulse of the movement. However the diversity, as well as the unity of a movement held together by the Charter itself, is increasingly being revealed by local studies of Chartism. In a society so unlike our own, unified as we are by the common experience of press, radio and television, the differences between one town and its neighbours were significant and expressed in the nature of local Chartism. But does this rich diversity lead inevitably to the conclusion that this was not a national movement but a collection of local grievances?

If Chartism was no more than localism given an occasional national face, was it also perhaps a movement of the working classes rather than a movement of the working class? Or was there a genuine unity and a sense of a shared class identity arising from the great divide imposed by the Reform Act of 1832 which parcelled English society into those with and those without property - on one side the enfranchised and on the other, the politically powerless?

Of the many questions that Chartism gives rise to, one that is open to many tentative answers relates to the sudden demise of the movement. Why did Chartism fade away so rapidly after 1848? Did Chartists despair of improvement by political action? Were they won over by the new individualism of the age, abandoning as useless baggage any sense of a common class interest? Another hypothesis suggests that the perceived impartiality of the State, as shown in such legislation as the Mines Act of 1842 which prohibited the employment of women and children underground, gave rise to the expectation that social improvement might come without the need for united working-class action.

Chartism was not the first association of working-class men. There had been others such as Friendly Societies, co-operatives and trade unions. Yet Chartism represented a major step forward in working-class movements: it was a national movement with a national leadership. At first, its objectives were narrowly political, with the expectation that after a successful campaign all else would follow. However, after its failure in 1848, the rump of the movement developed a socialist programme. Again, some Chartists took a different path and went on to become members of those Reform Associations which helped to pave the way for the extension of the franchise in late Victorian England. But perhaps the true significance of Chartism lies not in any influence it may have had on such developments but rather in offering the first example of an organised working-class party, equipped with a party programme, which fought elections, petitioned governments and sought to raise political awareness in its fight for political justice?

References
1   Frederick Engels, *The Condition of the Working Class in England* (Panther, 1972), p. 255.
2   Dorothy Thompson, *The Chartists* (Temple Smith, 1982), p. 2.
3   Ibid, pp. 2-3.

Studying 'Chartism'

This introductory chapter is intended to give you a broad overview of the subject and, together with the Chronological Table (pages 133-5), should enable you to familiarise yourself with key dates and some of the issues which arise from any study of this unprecedented political movement. At this stage it is important to see that although Chartism was a cyclical movement - like that of the British economy itself - and therefore had its peaks, it also had an underlying continuity rooted in a working-class culture which knit the movement together.

Part of that culture was an alternative interpretation of British history quite distinct from that familiar to middle- and upper-class Britain. It had its own gallery of heroes, in which Wellington or Nelson were replaced by radical thinkers such as Tom Paine or William Cobbett. It also had its martyrs in those slain at 'Peterloo' or transported from Tolpuddle. In the Chartist interpretation, the land was the people's, the workers were the sole creators of wealth and the 1832 Reform Act was not the great leap forward which at first sight it might seem but rather a fraud imposed upon the majority of the nation by a repressive government.

This chapter can do no more than sketch the general outlines of the movement. Read Chapter 2 if you wish to look in more detail at its origins and Chapter 3 for an account of the First Petition in 1839. The history of the subsequent Petitions is examined in Chapters 5 and 6. If you prefer, you could leave Chapter 4 which examines the background of Chartism until you've studied the way the movement developed and declined. Chapter 7 considers the final years and Chapter 8 its decline and the historical controversies which surround the movement.

2 The Origins of Chartism

The decade of the 1830s was a period of great significance in the history of working-class movements in Britain. It began with the agitation for political reform and the passing of the Reform Act of 1832 and ended with the first Chartist petition in 1839. Within that short period of time, the working class, often with wider class support, were involved in many movements to secure social change and improvement. These ranged from agitation against 'reforms' such as the Poor Law Amendment Act of 1834 to demands for legislation to control working hours in the factories. This chapter will examine the relationship between these different movements and the development of Chartism and consider how far the limited reform of 1832 and the subsequent policies of the Whig government were responsible for contemporary discontents.

1 A Changing Society

The pace of economic change in our own time, the speed with which new industries grow and old ones decay, has had a profound effect on our society, for instance transforming confident mining communities into villages with high unemployment, replacing long-term employment with short-term contracts, unsettling long-established career expectations. The effects of these changes are clearly visible around us: the consequences are very much the subject of debate. What is not in dispute is that these economic changes which run so deep do affect us all. Against this background, politicians strive hard to create the 'feel good' factor - in short the reflection of better times - to demonstrate the success of their own policies.

In a not dissimilar way, the Chartist decades, the 30s and 40s of the nineteenth century, were times of rapid change, of economic growth and decay. The most obvious signs were the development of new forms of machinery in the textile industry, which in turn depended on the availability of different sources of power, first water and then steam.

The increasing use of steam depended on the availability of coal as a fuel to heat the water. The new factories and factory towns, therefore, were of necessity built near coal faces. The factory, with its rigid discipline, its clamour, its heavy day of toil, increasingly replaced the domestic hearth as the main centre for textile production. However, this change-over should not be overstressed for by 1851 only six per cent of the workforce in England and Wales worked in factories, and most of those in small factories employing fewer than 100.

The new textile, cotton, had two important advantages over wool, the traditional all-purpose fabric: it was cheaper and easier to wash. Domestic and then overseas demand for this new fabric grew very rapidly. By the time of the Chartists, cotton cloth was being exported to Latin America, Asia and Africa, as well as to Europe. The expansion of the market helped to revolutionise production, and in Lancashire the cotton industry reached boom proportions. One obvious sign of this change was the growth of new towns, symbolised by Manchester, seen by contemporaries as the typical new industrial town, with its squalid jumble of factories and slums, contrasting sharply with the traditional English market town or cathedral city, weathered by centuries, with its slums more discreetly shielded from the visitor's gaze. By 1851, there were seven such towns in England, all with populations over 100,000, still small in comparison with London which had two million inhabitants in a total British population of 18.5 million.

The effect of a market economy was also a novelty in these years of Chartist activity. In the past, in traditional society, the yield of the harvest and the consequent price of corn, the basic element in the cost of living, tended to be the main factor affecting the life of the poor. In the new economic conditions, although the price of corn was still significant, the ability to sell the new manufactures, principally cotton goods, to Britain's growing population, and most importantly, the need to export to a world market, became of increasing importance. If buyers were unwilling or unable to buy, the effect on factory production was immediate and disastrous. If the 'market' failed, that is if there was insufficient demand, the consequence was a 'slump', with lay-offs and instant distress in the manufacturing districts. If, on the other hand, there was a strong demand, there would be a 'boom', with full and expanding employment. During the Chartist years, the emerging new-style capitalist economy was continually plagued by the see-saw nature of the market, by boom and slump.

Contemporaries, such as the Methodist preacher, J.R. Stephens, pointed to the direct relationship between a full belly and political protest in his famous claim that 'Universal Suffrage was a knife and fork question'. That the main periods of Chartist activity coincided with periods of economic downturn has been demonstrated by Professor W.W. Rostow in his 'social tension chart' based on bread prices and statistics of economic activity.[1] The years 1837-42 and 1847-8 were, in this analysis, periods of high tension, which adds support to Stephens's claim. However, such an apparently direct link between distress and political activity should not lead to a simplistic assessment of Chartism as no more than a protest against bad times or the assumption that the absence of protest was a reflection of the 'feel good' factor. Perhaps the sense of injustice generated by the denial of the vote simply became more acute in times of economic distress, as Chartists linked their exclusion from political power to their inability to create a more just society. Given the vote, times for working men, they argued, would of necessity be better, for with political power they would then be able to get a fairer share of the fruits of their labour.

2 The Radical Tradition

When in August 1838, at the mass meeting on Newhall Hill, Birmingham, the Chartists presented a programme based on political rights and an end to taxation without representation, there already existed a common stock of ideas on which they could draw and a strong tradition of political campaigning developed over many years. Central to Chartism was the concept of equality based on the fundamental right to vote. There was no novelty in this, but why, it must be asked, did this demand surface so vigorously in the 1830s? Were there any special circumstances which gave it fresh urgency? The answer, perhaps is, as Edward Royle claims, because 'by the late 1830s a radical working-class presence existed in all the industrial areas of Britain'.[2]

That the vote was a fundamental right that all should have was first effectively voiced in the 1770s by Thomas Cartwright in his pamphlet *Take Your Choice* published in 1776, the year of America's Declaration of Independence, a time in which long-established forms of government were coming under fierce scrutiny. Thomas Paine, one of England's greatest radical writers, took up the call in *The Rights of Man* (1791) in which he argued that the franchise was a natural right belonging to all men. During the long wars against Revolutionary France in the 1790s, when fearful of the contagion of revolution the British government became steadily more repressive, Paine was forced into exile. However, his ideas became part of the intellectual heritage of that radical working-class movement which flowered in the years immediately after the end of the war in 1815.

From a quite different standpoint, William Cobbett, ploughboy, pamphleteer and, finally, Member of Parliament, was successor to Paine. Cobbett saw himself as a true Englishman, anxious only to wrest power from the corrupt money grubbers who then ruled England, and to return that power to the people themselves. His call for parliamentary reform in the *Political Register*, his radical newsheet, in 1816 became a rallying cry in the Northern towns and villages and spurred on the Hampden Clubs (named after the famous opponent of Charles I's tax policies) to petition and campaign for the right to vote.

In the less repressive atmosphere of post-war Britain, both press and pressure groups flourished, with Lancashire weavers leading the way with a demand for manhood suffrage. A traditional form of political protest was the procession. This consisted of workers and their families, usually armed with banners setting out their demands, walking in orderly lines from the surrounding villages to the centre of the local town. There they would assemble to listen to a political address from the 'hustings', a make-shift platform set up in the town square. Such a meeting organised on 16 August 1819, in St Peter's Fields, Manchester, ended in tragedy.

The speaker was Henry 'Orator' Hunt, a gentleman radical, the most famous platform speaker of the day, of whom Feargus O'Connor, the Chartist leader, was a direct intellectual descendant. The local magistrates ordered the yeomanry - basically Manchester manufacturers on horseback - into the crowd to arrest Hunt. This ill-judged decision resulted in the death of 11 and injury to more than 600. It also gave a new word to the language, 'Peterloo', a grimly sardonic reference to another less unequal occasion, the recent battle of Waterloo. The events of that day stayed long in working-class memory and, as Royle and Walvin point out, 'helped feed the hostility of working-class reformers to the government and the social class from which the yeomanry were recruited'.[3] The immediate response of Lord Liverpool's Tory government was to pass the Six Acts (1819) of which the most oppressive was that which imposed a heavy stamp duty on newspapers so as to push the price of radical papers such as Cobbett's out of the reach of working-class readers.

3 The 1832 Reform Act

If 'Peterloo' was seen as direct evidence of what government was capable of, then the 1832 Reform Act seemed further evidence of ruling-class hostility to working-class political ambitions. Working-class radicals argued that they, too, had played a significant part in that extra-parliamentary pressure which kept out the Tories and secured the safe passage of the Third Reform Bill. Yet as a class they were still denied the vote, and were without political rights. As a consequence, they readily saw the 1832 Act as the first stage in the great 'Whig betrayal' which underpinned working-class political thinking in the 1830s. But was this interpretation justified by a course of events which seemed often to take the form of an increasingly acrimonious wrangle within a governing class bedevilled by the need to tinker with the ancient constitution, sacrosanct to most Tories, so as to pacify opinion outside Parliament yet without unduly distressing or disadvantaging its own members?

The crisis began in November 1830 and lasted until June 1832. During this time Parliament and country were dominated by the clamour for reform. The electoral system where votes and boroughs could be bought and sold was openly corrupt and the electoral map long since outdated. When the Duke of Wellington's Tory government fell (after the Duke had fulsomely praised the existing electoral arrangements), Lord Grey took office, heading a Whig administration manned almost entirely by the aristocracy. The Reform Bill crisis proper began with the introduction in March 1831 of the First Reform Bill and ended with the passing of the Third Reform Bill by the Lords in June 1832. Its passage was marked by a fierce struggle between Commons and Lords and by bitter divisions within the Commons itself. The First Reform Bill, introduced by Lord Russell,

was not the fine tuning that members had anticipated but a comprehensive reform of all the major abuses. One fundamental reform,
Lord Durham's proposal for a secret ballot, was rejected at the
drafting stage as undermining landowners' control of their tenants'
votes.

The Commons passed Russell's Bill but only by a single vote. With
minor changes, Russell re-introduced the Bill but, faced by Tory criticism of some clauses, the Whigs went to the country and fought an
election on the single issue of parliamentary reform. They were
returned, with a clear mandate for reform. A second Bill was introduced and passed the Commons with a majority of 136 but in October
1831 was defeated in the Lords by a majority of 41.

Faced by this impasse, the Whigs brought in a third Bill which
passed with a majority of 162. In the Lords, it secured a narrow
majority, but was then amended in a manner unacceptable to the
government. Grey sought to persuade the King, William IV, to use the
Crown's traditional power, the royal prerogative, to create 50 or more
peers to secure its safe passage. When the King refused, the Whigs
resigned, on 9 May. For six days the country was without a government as Wellington sought to patch together a Tory administration.
In the event, he was unsuccessful and he advised the King to recall
Lord Grey. William then accepted the necessity of creating sufficient
Whig peers but rather than see their numbers swelled by upstarts, the
Lords then passed the Bill. The Reform Bill crisis was at an end.

Dorothy Thompson sums up what people had thought had
happened:

> Faced with popular pressure, a corrupt Parliament, based on patronage
> and interest, had voluntarily extended its privileges to a section of the
> hitherto unenfranchised.[4]

This assessment, that the people had forced the hand of the government, was widely accepted and was a significant factor in much political discontent in the next two decades. To the Chartists, it pointed
the way forward. But does the historical record now support this view?

Certainly three English cities, it seemed, had played a major part in
the events which led up to the passing of the Bill: Birmingham, Bristol
and London itself. In Birmingham, a city with a social and economic
structure based on small workshops, and, in consequence, with a
closer relationship between worker and employer than in Manchester
or in any other of the northern mill towns, the Birmingham Political
Union (BPU) had emerged as a cross-class alliance between the
middle and working class. Its leader was a wealthy local banker,
Thomas Attwood. In the Reform Bill crisis, the BPU led the popular
demand for reform of Parliament, and Birmingham and Attwood
himself were seen as speaking for the country as a whole. In Bristol,
political protest had taken a quite different form. In October 1831,
rioters had set fire to the town centre and by the end of the distur-

bances possibly more than 400 people were dead or injured. Similar but less serious disturbances had taken place in Derby and Nottingham. These riots were sparked off by the rejection of the Second Reform Bill by the House of Lords. In its aftermath, the BPU let it be known that they intended to form an armed civic guard, ostensibly to protect the city. It is Derek Fraser's view that this was 'perhaps of greater importance than any of its other actions'.[5] This threat of an armed force which might be the spearhead of revolutionary activity spurred the Cabinet to introduce a further Bill. Attwood then dropped his threat.

When the Third Reform Bill was sent to the Lords and the King rejected Grey's request for more Whig peers, Grey's resignation on 9 May plunged the country into its deepest crisis. The Duke of Wellington was notorious in his opposition to reform and a Tory government under his leadership now seemed certain. These were the' Days of May' which some historians have seen as bringing Britain to the brink of revolution. In the critical 'Days of May', political unions multiplied, and Attwood in Birmingham mounted a campaign to force the government's hand and talked once more of taking up arms.

In London, the agitation was headed by Francis Place, one of the most famous radicals of the day, who called for the withdrawal of funds from the Bank of England with the slogan 'To stop the Duke, go for gold', intended to undermine the banking system and to intensify the trade recession which followed Grey's resignation. His overall purpose was to bring financial and economic pressure to bear on the government. There were also plans for an armed resistance if a new Tory administration was formed.

A London-based working-class political association was formed, the National Union of the Working Classes, which had a programme based upon the Rights of Man, on universal suffrage and on the necessity of resisting governments which 'violate the rights of the people'. However, its numbers were small, no more than 20,000. Certainly in the crisis of 1830-32, working class radicalism made itself heard and, in London, quite independently of the middle class. But revolutionary working-class activity as distinct from revolutionary rhetoric was not a force in the politics of the time.

What did affect Grey and the Whigs (but not Wellington) was the willingness of middle-class radicals such as Attwood and Place to suggest confrontation, and therefore civil war. As Michael Brock stresses: 'They meant to threaten a revolution, not to make one'.[6] Middle-class politicking was indeed a significant influence on the minds of the Whig cabinet, urging them towards a goal much desired. Armed rebellion was threatened if Wellington, the arch opponent of reform, patched together a government. But Wellington's hopes were destroyed by Robert Peel's refusal to join any government prepared to consider reform, as Wellington secretly was. Peel's obstinacy prevented the formation of a Tory government, thus paving the way for the return of the Whigs. In the final analysis, then, Wellington was defeated not by the country but by his own divided Tory party, which would not form up behind him. On their side the Whigs wanted reform, a final settlement, so the political unions were pushing at an open door.

If the Reform Act is examined in terms of what it set out to achieve rather than how it reached the statute book, it might well be seen as a betrayal. For the Whig historian, Thomas Babington Macaulay, it was a judicious measure, clearly designed to maintain political stability by extending the definition of 'property' to include other than landed property, thereby enfranchising the middle class, the famous £10 householder, defined as the owner or tenant of a house with a yearly rental value of £10. Subsequent historians have viewed it rather differently as a means of strengthening the power of the landed class. In this they agree with Grey's description of the Bill as: 'the most aristocratic measure that was ever proposed in Parliament'. Two aspects of 1832 justify this verdict: there were to be more county MPs - traditionally controlled by the aristocracy and gentry - and the 'Chandos' clause which gave the vote to the £50 tenants-at-will, that is to those tenants who could summarily be turned off their farm by their aristocratic landlord if they voted against his wishes.

However, the inner workings of the political system were screened from the public at large and it was generally accepted that the 'people' had defeated the Tories and thereby secured the passing of the Reform Act. In consequence, there was a readiness to see 1832 as a first step, an instalment leading inevitably to further reform. New campaigns, renewed pressure, more petitions would result in similar revolutionary changes. In such a way was the myth of 1832 born. For the aristocratic Whigs, it was intended was to bring the property-owning middle classes, those with a 'stake in the country,' into a defensive alliance, thereby dividing the haves from the have-nots. In this way they were wholly successful: the once radical middle class, newly-enfranchised, became natural conservatives.

4 Allies and Fellow Travellers

What the Reform agitation had given to the working class was experience in organisation and in campaigning. It would not, however, be true to claim that it politicised the working class although it clearly helped to carry on the process which had begun in the troubled years after the Napoleonic Wars. One major force had been William Cobbett's *Political Register* which had not only informed its readers of the need for reform but had spurred them on to take part in political meetings or in the good-humoured but determined processions characteristic of the time. Yet another potent influence was the campaign for the Unstamped Press. In an attempt to stifle papers such as

Cobbett's, the government in 1819 had imposed a tax on all newspapers with the aim of destroying the radical press by making their newspapers too dear for the working class to buy. This act of censorship had been met by the publication of unstamped (and therefore illegal) newspapers of which the most influential was the *Poor Man's Guardian*, first appearing in 1831, published by Henry Hetherington, with editor Bronterre O'Brien, subsequently one of the most distinguished of Chartist theorists. The *Poor Man's Guardian* stood foursquare behind the demand for universal suffrage. Other newspapers both in London and in the provinces began to circulate and an underground network of sellers and publishers was created which, despite prison sentences imposed on publishers and sellers, continued to operate until 1835 when the stamp duty was reduced

Edward Royle comments that 'a generation of radical leaders cut its teeth on the struggle'.[7] And indeed a direct link can be traced between this campaign and the origins of the Charter itself. Working-class members of the London-based Society for the Promotion of the Repeal of the Stamp Duties formed in 1836 the Association of Working Men to procure a Cheap and Honest Press. In the same year, this evolved into the London Working Men's Association, which nevertheless allowed non-working-class sympathisers to become honorary members. It was this cross-class alliance, made up of the Association and six honorary members, all MPs, which on 31 May 1837 set out the Six Points of that Charter which was to give the Chartists their name - and purpose.

If the existence of a radical working-class press in the early 1830s was a means by which working-class political consciousness was raised, so also, argues Dorothy Thompson, was the 1833 Irish Coercion Act, introduced to deal with increasing agrarian violence in Ireland. It was, she says, 'a most essential ingredient in the development of Chartism'.[8] This Act gave draconian powers to the Irish local authorities to suppress most kinds of political activity including ordinary political meetings and to establish a curfew in any district declared 'disturbed' with courts martial replacing the ordinary civilian courts. To working-class radicals, this Act, one of the first of the new Parliament, was seen as a warning of the shape of things to come in Britain itself, and prompted them to offer support to the leader of the Irish parliamentary party, Daniel O'Connell. O'Connell was to be one of the signatories of the Charter itself but this link was broken by O'Connell's opposition to trade unionism and by the split between O'Connell and Feargus O'Connor, the most influential of all the Chartist leaders. The new government's Irish policy provoked mass meetings in Birmingham and Manchester, on a par with those earlier reform meetings, protesting against the threat to Irish (and English) liberties posed by this statute.

5 Trade Unionism

Trade unions had existed before the 1830s but were found mainly amongst printers and engineers and in mining communities in Yorkshire and South Wales. These were the fore-runners of the so-called 'labour aristocracy', workers whose special skills gave them clout in the labour market. Factory-based industry brought the growth of a new working class in the northern manufacturing districts, comprising semi-skilled and un-skilled operatives, with little or no bargaining power.

In the recent past, as early as 1818, there had been short-lived attempts to bring such workers into loose trade associations such as the 'Philanthropic Hercules' in London and, in Lancashire, the 'Philanthropic Society'. John Doherty's Cotton Spinners Union, founded in Manchester in 1829, was initially more successful. From his Lancashire base, he recruited Staffordshire potters and then expanded into the creation of a more general union, the National Association for the Protection of Labour, which lasted until 1832 and at its height had members in the Midlands and in Yorkshire.

The culmination of attempts to form a general union was clearly the Grand National Consolidated Trades Union (GNCTU). This must be seen not only as within the sequence which began in 1818, but primarily within the context of the 1830s as forming part of that wider working-class movement reflected in a whole range of activities, from political reform groups to Short-time Committees (see page 17). New industries, new towns, new forms of action, and new hopes helped produce the Grand National in 1834.

The GNCTU arose from a call for help sent by Derby trade unionists to fellow workers in London when faced by intransigent employers determined to stamp out trade unions in the local trades. Their call was answered by the summoning of a conference from which the GNCTU was formed. This short-lived universal union (which lasted only six months) has often been seen as an attempt to put into practice the ideas of Robert Owen, the industrialist and philanthropist, and a profound critic of the new social order that the machine was creating.

By any standard, Robert Owen was a remarkable man. Born in 1771 at Newtown, Montgomeryshire, the son of a postmaster, he rose by his native energy and a judicious marriage to be the owner of textile mills at New Lanark, south of Glasgow, which he had bought from his father-in-law. Owen's fundamental criticism of the values he saw emerging from industrialisation was formulated in 1817 in *A New View of Society*, in which he sketched his vision of a new society based on co-operation. Man's whole environment, he argued, should be so changed that he would shed his competititive characteristics and work in harmony with his fellow man for humanity's improvement. At his factory, through enlightened educational and welfare schemes, Owen

tried to create such an environment. At this time, European philoso-
phers were much excited by the possibility of moulding human
nature afresh, and his social experiments attracted reformers from all
over the continent. In capitalist society, Owen recognised that the
principle of co-operation would imply comprehensive unionisation
which in turn would imply alternative means by which industry could
be organised. Mutualism (working together for the common good)
would replace competition.

In the six months of its active life in 1834, the GNCTU had relatively few members, around 16,000, but it had a large body of sympathisers. The GNCTU was Owenite in that it shared Robert Owen's
enthusiasm for co-operation but it was also concerned with members'
wages in their own industries. During its short life, it spawned many
ideas, from co-operative work schemes to land settlements. Despite its
name, it was more local - mainly amongst the London tailors and
shoemakers - than national. As W.H. Fraser remarks: 'it was less a
culmination of the general union, as so often assumed, than merely
the London section'.[9]

The State took immediate and repressive action when, in rural
Dorset, agricultural labourers set up a branch of the GNCTU in
Tolpuddle. This invasion of the countryside by the GNCTU was seen
by the Whig government as a too direct threat to the established
order in the then troubled conditions of rural England and conjured
up government's persistent nightmare of urban militants politicising
the rural population. *The Times* called for action, and Melbourne, the
Home Secretary, invoked a 1797 statute against unlawful oaths and, as
a consequence, six luckless labourers in Dorset were sentenced to
seven years' transportation. The country rang with trade union
protest and London saw the first massive trade union demonstration,
a cavalcade of workers carrying a petition to the Prime Minister. The
'Tolpuddle Martyrs' gave clear evidence of the repressive means the
State would use against undesirable associations of working men.

6 The Factory Movement

One campaign which had left its mark upon the moral imagination of
the nation was the abolitionist movement which had triumphed in the
Act for Emancipation passed in 1833, setting free all the slaves in the
Empire. The crusade for abolition had brought together a motley
band of interests running from evangelicals and liberal-minded MPs
to industrialists opposed to the high price of West Indian sugar. The
movement to restrict the hours of 'slaves' in the factories called forth
similar emotions and drew in groups and individuals almost as widely
different in commitment and background. Prominent as leaders were
Churchmen and Tories; at the base were Short-time Committees,
pressure groups to limit factory working hours, formed in all the main
manufacturing districts of Lancashire and Yorkshire and composed

principally of working men. In this sense the Factory Movement was another way in which the new urban classes were politicised and were given organising and campaigning experience. It was also yet another aspect of that general discontent which marked post-Reform Britain.

Although the Factory Movement shared the same sense of moral outrage which powered the evangelical abolitionists, it differed from that first successful crusade in one fundamental way. 'Freeing the slaves' was a demand in tune with the times, with the call from freedom from restrictions, the sweeping away of state controls. The liberal doctrine was based upon the assumption that *laissez-faire*, the absence of all unnecessary controls on human or collective action, was in the general interest of all. It was believed that each person was the best protector of his or her own interest. To oppose that doctrine, which was the engine of capitalist society, by calling for legislation to protect factory children was to earn the epithet of 'humanity-monger', the nineteenth century equivalent of 'do-gooder'.

There had been earlier attempts to limit the hours of factory children - notably by Sir Robert Peel, a Tory factory owner and father of Robert Peel, who became Prime Minister - but these laws had depended upon a lax local magistracy for enforcement and consequently were largely evaded. It was not until 1830 that the campaign began in earnest and became a genuine national movement. At the heart of the movement in the 1830s were Tory politicians such as Michael Sadler and Lord Ashley (later Lord Shaftesbury). The organising genius of the movement in the country was Richard Oastler, a Tory land agent. It would be easy to see the movement in terms of traditionalist land-owning Tories pitted against the new go-ahead manufacturers, committed to profits and cost effectiveness. However, landowners could be found siding with the manufacturing interest, while some industrialists sympathised with the need to regulate hours. Robert Owen, of course, was one of these, but there were others such as John Fielden of Todmorden. Another was John Wood, a Bradford Tory manufacturer, who was to play a leading part in the campaign.

The national movement began in earnest when John Wood wrote in 1830 to the Leeds *Mercury* on 'Yorkshire slavery', describing the Bradford mills as 'magazines of British infantile slavery'. This was the trigger which sent Oastler into action and prompted the setting up of Short-time Committees in the four main Yorkshire mill towns. Oastler then went on to call on workers to 'establish committees in every manufacturing town and village, to collect information and publish facts'. His call was answered in all the textile districts, where committees were set up, manned by workers and tradesmen, financed by gentry, clergy and sympathetic manufacturers, with additional funding from Wood and Oastler. From his base near Huddersfield, Oastler made missionary tours throughout the manufacturing areas, intent on raising public awareness of 'the horrors of the system'. He gave leadership to a campaign which seemed again to demonstrate that popular pressure could affect the policy of governments. In 1833, Lord Ashley, the parliamentary leader of the movement, secured the passing of a Factory Act which produced a fundamental change in that it not only regulated children's hours but established a state inspectorate to oversee its workings. This Act was not judged the final word by the Short-time Committees but as a stage towards a more effective control which would benefit adult workers as well as children.

Although the Factory Movement was active for the next two decades, after 1834 its grass roots supporters were caught up first in the Anti-Poor Law Campaign (in which Oastler was a major player) and then in Chartism itself, which held the promise of an end to all working-class grievances. When the Factory Movement was at its height all the techniques later to become familiar in Chartism were deployed: mass meetings and itinerant lecturers, rallies on the moors, petitioning and pamphleteering. What it fostered above all was working-class enthusiasm to give time and energy to bring about much needed reform.

7 The Anti-Poor Law Campaign

The 1834 Poor Law Amendment Act was intended to deal with the increasing burden on the rates posed by the rural poor and to put an end to what was widely seen as the waste and inefficiency of the Old Poor Law system. This was administered by the local authorities, the JPs, and was based upon the parish, whose duty it was to decide rates of relief, who was eligible and, if need be, to build and maintain a workhouse. In place of the old parish system, the New Poor Law was to group parishes together in a Union, empowered to build a workhouse, run by locally elected boards of guardians, with overall control given to a central body, the Poor Law Commission. The intention was to end the system of 'outdoor relief', the system by which those living on the parish were allowed to stay in their homes rather than being forced into a workhouse.

'Outdoor relief' was widely seen as an increasingly heavy burden on the rates and the 1834 Act was designed to end this practice. Under the new rules, applicants for parish assistance were to undergo the 'workhouse test' and to be offered a place in newly-built Union workhouses. A rejection of this offer was indicative that the applicant was not in genuine need. Conditions in the workhouse were to be based upon the 'principle of less eligibility', a reflection of the political philosophy of Jeremy Bentham, the most famous thinker of the day. Bentham stated that human behaviour was based on a simple principle: men and women sought pleasure and avoided pain. Therefore, if conditions in the workhouse were 'less eligible', that is more painful, than the worst conditions outside, workhouse inmates would be goaded into finding work. The workhouse, constructed on this

Benthamite principle, would benefit all: paupers would find work; ratepayers would save money. The theory had one major short-coming: it assumed that work was there to be found.

That this measure was singularly inappropriate to an industrial society where short-term unemployment was the norm was only one of many defects of the 1834 Act. And again it was a paradox that a House of Commons generally opposed to state intervention and central control (as the debates on Factory Reform had shown) should pass a Bill which replaced local liberties by a centrally-appointed and unelected body. In the Commons, the Bill came under fire from William Cobbett and from John Walter, MP for Berkshire. Walter was also the proprietor of *The Times*, which was to become one of the main opponents of the New Poor Law. Outside Parliament, opposition was directed at two very different aspects. Tories such as Richard Oastler saw it as striking at the roots of traditional society, replacing a social order bound together by common ties of duty and responsibility with a centralised system with no local roots. For working men and women on the other hand, the issue was seen more starkly: as another instance of the war of the propertied classes against ordinary men and women.

In many different parts of the country the Poor Law Commission was met with hostility but only in Lancashire and the West Riding of Yorkshire was opposition persistent and widespread. Here riots and disturbance marked the arrival of the hated Poor Law Commissioners. The northern parishes prided themselves on their efficiency and cost-effectiveness, and so when the Poor Law Commission arrived in 1836 with plans to amalgamate parishes into Unions, they were faced by opposition not only from workers but, to their great surprise, from some of the local notables as well.

The time chosen could not have been worse, for it was the beginning of a downturn in the economic cycle. The objections raised turned not only on the impossibility of providing workhouse accommodation for the mass of the unemployed but on the cost to the ratepayer. Outdoor relief, they argued, gave cheap temporary assistance. The new workhouse system had no relevance to short-term unemployment in industrial society. To force workers to sell up all their worldly goods, their furniture and fittings, would condemn them to a lifetime of misery with little prospect of setting up home again.

These and similar arguments were voiced by local JPs, such as John Fielden of Todmorden (who had been a leader in the Factory Movement), and by members of the clergy, like Patrick Brontë of Haworth (father of the Brontë sisters, the famous novelists). Local manufacturers, too, were hostile, prominent amongst them Edward Ashworth, a Bolton cotton mill owner. Amongst factory workers feeling ran high, fanned by atrocity stories of workhouse treatment which rivalled those describing pre-emancipation slave conditions.

The techniques used to organise protest were identical to those of other campaigns such as the Factory Movement. Central was the public meeting, chaired by a local dignitary, with a key-note speech delivered by a visiting speaker. One important purpose of the meeting was to collect signatures to a petition sent to Parliament demanding an end to interference from the hated Commissioners. The high point of any local campaign would be a mass meeting such as that at Hartshead Moor in the West Riding on Whit Tuesday, 1837, when Oastler himself was the main speaker.

The press played an important part. Many Northern newspapers such as the *Leeds Intelligencer* or the *Bolton Chronicle* were prepared to support the agitation by giving coverage to the meetings and by publishing hostile accounts of the work of the Commission. When, in November 1837, Feargus O'Connor began publishing the *Northern Star*, a new and powerful voice was added to the campaign. In London, *The Times* under John Walter continued to maintain its initial hostility to the 1834 Act. So widespread and so intense was opposition in Lancashire and the West Riding of Yorkshire that by 1838 government backed down. Postponement became general and Commissioners formally instructed the northern counties Poor Law authorities to continue to work within the pre-existing rules. The movement peaked in 1838 and then began to decline. The reasons for this falling away are diverse. For the temporary unemployed, relief did not mean the dreaded workhouse; those in need found that the poor law was still administered in the traditional way. Working-class energies, therefore, were readily diverted into Chartism with its radiant hopes of more fundamental change. Tory opponents of the New Poor Law resented the loss of this grass-roots support to a different movement with which they had little sympathy and, as a consequence, local campaign committees split apart. The parish authorities continued largely undisturbed in their old ways. The impetus was lost, and although the Act remained unrepealed, local victory proved sufficient to damp down the bitter antagonisms.

8 Conclusion

The 1830s, then, had witnessed the emergence of a diverse range of protest campaigns, many of which had in common a disenchantment either with the new legislation of the newly-reformed Parliament or, as in the case of the Factory Reform Movement, with the failure to protect the weakest in society. The campaigns were all wholly peaceful, conducted in press, meeting hall and in *ad hoc* organisations. They had brought together widely different social classes in a common cause. And again only in Ireland, still not seen as an equal part of the United Kingdom, had special powers been imposed. The threat to British institutions as a whole which this Act seemed to imply was never realised. Government indeed behaved with some circumspection. Only when faced by the stirrings of discontent in rural England, seen as threat to its own class interests, did government wield the heavy stick of transportation. What the decade had offered was an immediate education in political action, particularly for the worker in the northern manufacturing districts.

What, then, was the relationship between Chartism and these previous campaigns, and in particular between Chartism and the Anti-Poor Law campaign? Mark Hovell, the first historian of the Chartist movement, summed up this connection in military terms, viewing the Anti-Poor Law campaigners as an army 'unwilling to disband without attacking somebody' and allowing 'itself to be led anywhere'.[10] James Epstein offers a more sympathetic and more perceptive assessment. He emphasises 'the merging of a defensive movement ... with a mass national movement'.[11] What quite clearly was left behind, indeed was handed on, was a conviction of the value of organised protest and a style of hell-fire oratory, both of which were to surface again in Chartism. And for some Chartists there remained the sense that violence or the threat of violence had helped win the battle.

However, in one very important respect, Chartism differed from all other movements of the time, in that it was proposing a revolutionary change in the political structure of Victorian Britain. Most previous campaigns had asked only for improvement, or, as in the case of the Anti-Poor-Law protest, a return to old and tried practices. Although the Reform Bill agitation seems, at first glance, to be analogous, it clearly was not. In that popular movement, the running was made by the ruling elite: there was a prior acceptance of the urgent need for change. The Chartists, however, confronted an almost entirely hostile establishment. Their demand for universal suffrage implied the transfer of political power to the 'people', striking at the very roots of a hierarchical society based on the rights of property. Chartism, in its assertion that 'the people are the source of all power', was to take a giant step forward from the campaigns of its forerunners.

References

1 W.W. Rostow, *British Economy of the Nineteenth Century* (Oxford University Press, 1948), p. 25.
2 Edward Royle, *Chartism*, (Longman, third edition 1996), p. 16.
3 Edward Royle and James Walvin, *English Radicals and Reformers 1760-1848*, (The Harvester Press, 1982), p. 119.
4 Dorothy Thompson, *The Chartists* (Temple Smith, 1984), p. 17.
5 Derek Fraser 'The Agitation for Parliamentary Reform' in *Popular Movements c.1830-1850* edited by J.T. Ward (Macmillan, 1970), p. 45.
6 Michael Brock, *The Great Reform Act* (Gregg Revivals, 1973), p. 309.
7 Royle, *Chartism*, p. 51.
8 Thompson, *The Chartists*, p. 19.
9 W.H. Fraser, 'Trade Unionism' in *Popular Movements*, p. 105.

10 Mark Hovell, *The Chartist Movement* (Manchester University Press, 1918), p. 98.
11 James Epstein, *The Lion of Freedom* (Croom Helm, 1982), p. 101.

Answering essay questions on 'The origins of Chartism'

Questions on this topic are:
1. 'Chartism was no more than a bundle of local discontents given a national face'. Discuss.
2. To what extent was Chartism simply a reaction to the Whig reforms of the 1830s?

Both these questions call for an understanding not only of the immediate causes of Chartism but also of its long term origins. It is important to confront the question and to select material that is directly related to the question as set and not to some other question for which you had prepared. Shape your answer so that each paragraph develops one main strand of your argument. In a sense, writing a good examination answer needs similar skills to those used by a barrister in preparing a brief.

There is no ideal answer to any question. What you must do is decide what point of view you wish to develop. If the topic is set in the form of a question, as in the second example, there is no need to agree with it. And again be mindful of the phrase 'to what extent' which requires you to make a judgement and to consider what other factors should be taken into account. Both these questions would allow you, if you wished, to draw on the political background of Chartism and to give weight to such factors as the Hampden Clubs or the political tradition represented by Tom Paine or William Cobbett.

The key to a good history essay is i) to construct an essay plan setting out the five or six main issues you intend to discuss, ii) to start with an opening paragraph which in broad outline shows how you intend to develop your argument, iii) in your answer to follow your plan, taking care to avoid a narrowly narrative approach for a high-scoring essay should be analytical and this is best done by supporting comments, assertions, or lines of argument with sound factual material which illustrate your sub-themes.

As an example of material which relates to either of these two questions, individual paragraphs could centre on:
a) the political tradition - Paine, Cobbett and the Hampden Clubs,
b) working-class involvement in the Reform Bill agitation and their subsequent exclusion from the franchise,
c) the impact of the expanding economy on the working class, citing examples such as the weavers,
d) social protest movements, in particular the campaign against the Poor Law Amendment Act and the Factory Movement,
e) the cross-class alliance - the LWMA, the BPU and the Charter.

In answering the first question, you would have an opportunity to consider how the origins of the movement differed so profoundly in different parts of Britain. In London artisans were building on their radical past; in Birmingham, manufacturers were anxious to wrest power from the country's ruling elite; and in the North and in Scotland quite different concerns powered the rise of Chartism. You may wish to emphasise its cross-class aspect, both in the LWMA and in the BPU, to illustrate the political origins, or you may prefer to see the general disappointment with Whig reforms as the principal driving force of a movement which was strongest in the manufacturing districts of the North of England. The argument that you present will very much depend on which factor or factors you think most important in accounting for the fusion of all these discontents into a national movement. A strongly-argued essay with a clearly-expressed point of view is often better than one which is equally balanced, provided of course that the evidence you use is both relevant and accurate.

Summary Diagram
The Origins of Chartism

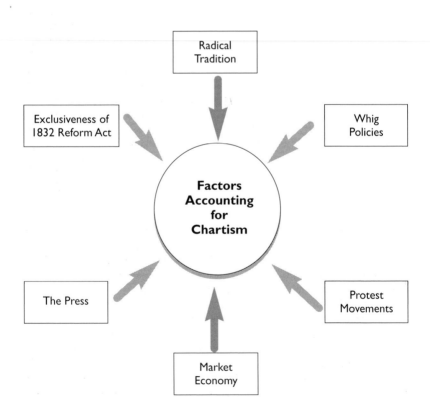

Radical Tradition

Exclusiveness of 1832 Reform Act

Whig Policies

Factors Accounting for Chartism

The Press

Protest Movements

Market Economy

3 The Chartist Movement in 1839

In the 1830s, anger and frustration, in great measure caused by that Reformed Parliament on which many had pinned such high hopes, helped to fuel protest movements calling for a reversal of policy. The form these movements took depended mainly on the social and economic context in which they arose. In the northern textile districts, some enlightened employers and Tory traditionalists, with mass support coming from the textile workers most at risk, called for the repeal of the hated new Poor Law. In London, the dominant campaigns were directed to repealing the stamp duty on newspapers, in essence to securing a free press, but above all to that demand for universal male suffrage which had been for so long an essential part of the radical tradition (see page 10).

What was so remarkable about the last years of the decade, 1838 and 1839, was the fusion of so many different - and widely-scattered - movements into one national campaign, the campaign for the Charter. Throughout the whole of the land, the call went forth to petition Parliament for a fundamental change in the Constitution. The petition was a time-honoured procedure to secure 'redress of grievances', that is to put right perceived wrongs. In the view of contemporary law-makers, the petition was the ultimate expression of the sovereignty of the people and was a force that no government could easily ignore. The Chartist movement, building on its supporters throughout the country, used this traditional means to submit the people's petition to Parliament in 1839. At the least this was a demonstration to the middle and upper classes of working-class ability to organise and present their political opinion to those in power. The petition also carried within it the popular conviction that all men were created equal and that that equality should be expressed in the right to vote. In the hierarchical, class-based society of Victorian Britain, the Chartist programme was a challenge to those who by reason of class wielded social and political power.

Furthermore, in the National Convention, the movement created a forum for Chartist opinion and an assembly within which strategy and tactics could be debated. The Chartist Convention must be seen for what at best it was: a representative body elected on a wider franchise than the House of Commons, where in an orderly fashion and following normal committee procedure the movement could debate how to secure the success of the Charter.

One question neither the movement in the country, nor the National Convention was able to solve: what the next move should be if the petition was rejected. To bear arms in self-defence was a time-honoured constitutional right but when could this right legitimately be invoked? Some Chartist leaders such as Feargus O'Connor hinted at the use of arms, using this as a tactic to bring pressure to bear on

Parliament and the established authorities. Others such as George Julian Harney looked to French Revolutionary precedent as the model to follow: a national rising to force the Charter into law. 1839 was to put to the test many such political theories and, as such, is a critical year not only in the history of Chartism but in the history of working-class movements in Britain.

1 William Lovett and London Working-class Radicalism

William Lovett was in his late thirties when he and the London Working Men's Association (LWMA) sprang into prominence with the publication of the Charter. Born in 1800 in Newlyn, in Cornwall, he had little formal education and at an early age he was apprenticed to his uncle's trade of rope-making. As this ancient trade began to decline, Lovett turned to carpentry and cabinet-making as an alternative. At the age of 21 he moved to London to seek his fortune.

In London, after a few years in the trade, Lovett became a member of the Cabinetmakers' Society and subsequently rose to be its president. London artisans had had a long radical tradition and Lovett, following a period of self-education, was drawn into the co-operative movement, the offspring of Owenism, and he became secretary to the British Association for the Promotion of Co-operative Knowledge, an Owenite society.

Lovett's work with Owenism marked the beginning of his increasingly active involvement in the radical movements of his time. When, in 1831, his friend Henry Hetherington (later a leading Chartist) defied the law requiring newspapers to pay a duty in the form of a stamp, and published the *Poor Man's Guardian* without paying the duty, Lovett became the secretary of the victims' committee set up to help support the families of those sent to prison for breaking the law. In the same year when like-minded radicals founded the National Union of the Working Classes (NUWC), both Lovett and Hetherington soon became members. Its declared purpose was to achieve universal suffrage, annual parliaments, the secret ballot, and the abolition of property qualifications for MPs, in essence the Chartist programme.

During the Reform Bill agitation (see page 11), Lovett was amongst those who urged arming in self-defence in anticipation of an expected attack. As I.J. Prothero stresses 'most radicals thought in terms of a continual increase in activity until there was a mass movement confronting the authorities',[1] a strategy similar to the doctrine of confrontation adopted by O'Connorite Chartists.

By the early 1830s, Lovett's intense involvement in radical causes had developed in him the skills which made him so successful as the initiator and draftsman of the Charter. He was an excellent committee man, democratic to the extreme in that he refused to accept leadership of any kind. What he lacked were the gifts of platform oratory, so essential in the democratic politics of his day. He was a man of great integrity, dedicated to the causes to which he devoted so much of his life, yet unable to command the people's affection and devotion earned so easily by Feargus O'Connor.

2 The London Working Men's Association

When in 1836 Lovett and his friends founded the London Working Men's Association (LWMA), it comprised around 100 fairly substantial artisans, with 35 honorary members. Its original purpose was educational - to provide a reading room, occasional lectures and regular discussions. However, the aims of the LWMA were never narrowly vocational but directed to the social and political emancipation of the class it represented. As the sole major radical working class association of the day, the LWMA attracted activists from a wide range of other groups, such as the Tolpuddle committee, trade unions and the co-operative movement and from the campaign for an unstamped press.

From its foundation, the LWMA rejected paternalism, i.e. the received wisdom that working men needed the guidance and leadership of the great and the good. To ensure its working-class stance and credentials, non-working men were excluded from the management committee so that the honorary members, men of standing and wealth, could never take over direction of its affairs. Like other radical organisations, the LWMA campaigned extensively on behalf of the transported Glasgow cotton spinners (see page 30). They also sent lecturers to the industrial districts of the North and the mining towns of South Wales to set up sister WMAs. Two of their most successful speakers were Henry Hetherington and Henry Vincent, another LWMA member who was to become an active Chartist. Their missionary tours in the North were hampered by a profound difference in background between LWMA members and their northern audiences. The 'Bastille' (as the workhouse was commonly known) held no threat for prosperous artisans as it did for workers in factories in Lancashire and Yorkshire, so the LWMA could not draw on that common stock of fear which helped fuel the rhetoric and the veiled threats of the anti-Poor Law campaigners. In this sense, as I. Prothero asserts, 'before 1839 London Chartism was virtually non-existent'[2] and despite the LWMA claim to authorship of the Charter, the running was made by O'Connor and his followers in the North.

3 The Charter

Chartism drew much of its strength from its provincial centres, particularly from the mill towns of Lancashire and Yorkshire, building on a framework established by the earlier popular movements of the 1830s. The Charter itself, however, was essentially the work of the metropolis, of the LWMA, of London artisans, together with sympathetic radical MPs. The name conjured up the medieval Magna Carta, seen as the victorious result of a struggle for liberty between people and king. The Charter, too, like its namesake, was to be an alternative constitution, a means by which an unjust and tyrannical government would be forced to accept change which the normal process of protest and petition had failed to achieve.

The call for universal suffrage had had a long history (see page 10) and had not been satisfied by the small-scale reform of 1832. When the London Working Men's Association was founded, one of its stated objects had been to carry forward the demand for the extension of the franchise and 'to seek by every legal means to place all classes of society in possession of their equal political and social rights'. This aim continued to dominate the discussions of the LWMA and, as early as October 1836, the LWMA had given support to five of what became the six points of the Charter.

On 31 May 1837, the LWMA called a meeting of its own members and of sympathetic radical MPs to consider what the next step should be. From this meeting came a joint committee of 12, six working men (including William Lovett, Henry Hetherington and Henry Vincent) and six MPs (Daniel O'Connell, J.A. Roebuck and W. Sharman Crawford amongst them) which on 7 June issued the statement of the Six Points. However, it was not until the following May that the document known as the People's Charter appeared, drawn up by William Lovett and Francis Place, master tailor and assiduous political organiser, an early example of a 'spin-doctor'. During the intervening period, three MPs had lost their seats in the 1837 General Election and a fourth, the Irish MP Daniel O'Connell, had antagonised working-class supporters by his advocacy of the 1834 Poor Law Amendment Act and his attack on trade unions. So even before the birth of the Chartist movement, the LWMA's crucial support and sponsors in Parliament had been seriously reduced.

Although the publication of the Charter in London went largely unnoticed in radical working-class circles in the North of England - mainly because its proposals were so familiar and formed part of a long-established radical tradition - in themselves the Six Points came to be seen as effectively summarising that tradition. Central to the Charter was the demand for the vote to be given to all men of 21 - and in effect the other clauses may be seen as a means by which that new power could be protected and nurtured. The secret ballot, rejected by the Whigs in 1832, was intended to prevent 'influence', such as the economic power held by landlords over tenant farmers, being used to limit free voting. The abolition of property qualications for MPs was to enable poor and rich alike to have access to the House of Commons. The fourth Point, the payment of MPs, had a similar purpose. The call for equal constituencies, by ensuring that each constituency had a broadly similar number of voters, was to make certain that each vote was equal in weight. The sixth Point, annual Parliaments, was to make MPs continuously responsible to the sovereign people by requiring them to seek a fresh mandate each year.

The LWMA's collaboration with Daniel O'Connell led to the resignation of some of its members, notably George Julian Harney, who formed a rival organisation, the East London Democratic Association, later re-named the London Democratic Association. This new association, whose radical credentials were declared by its birth-date, 29 January, the birthday of Thomas Paine, shared with Feargus O'Connor the firm conviction that the struggle for the Charter would ultimately be successful. To O'Connor, furthermore, it provided a useful link with London radicalism and an alternative to the LWMA, tainted now in his eyes by its continuing tolerance of the Irish leader.

A sweeping distinction is often made between the London radicals in the LWMA and the northern wing of what became the Chartist movement: London, it is claimed, was committed to moral force and opposed to violence in contrast to the northern campaigners, who considered violence, physical force, as the ultimate weapon. Yet this broad generalisation has to be treated with some caution for in London, too, the right to bear arms and to defend liberty against attacks by the state was generally accepted. What London radicals were anxious to avoid was the needless provocation of the established authorities, of the kind which typified Joseph Rayner Stephens, the Methodist preacher (see page 35).

4 The Revival of the Birmingham Political Union

The central role which Birmingham had played in the Reform Bill agitation was repeated - at least initially - in the origins of the Chartist movement. Thomas Attwood, wealthy Birmingham banker and member of Parliament, had been the BPU's prime mover in the Reform Bill crisis and from the post-1832 Parliament he had expected much - in particular the adoption of his own currency reform proposals, turning on the abandonment of the gold standard, which he saw as a burden on the small businesses on which the prosperity of Birmingham depended. When no such change in monetary policy occurred, and as depression once more hit Birmingham and the surrounding Black Country, he set about re-establishing the BPU with the intention of pushing for further political reform, not universal suffrage but household suffrage.

From the outset, however, Attwood's political position differed profoundly from that of O'Connor and the LWMA. Instinctively a Tory, he believed in 'virtual representation', in effect that working-class interests could safely be left in middle-class hands, and that 'the economic dominance of the manufacturer, merchant and banker over the "productive class" best fitted them to represent the whole of that class'.[3] Symptomatic of this approach was the social constitution of the ruling Political Council of the BPU. Of the 35 members of this, the BPU's ruling body, none was a working man. In Attwood's political army, leaders by right must be men of wealth and influence. A Political Council member, the industrialist G.F. Muntz, had defined the purpose of the BPU campaign as 'extending the franchise so as to enable them to return to the House of Commons a majority of men of business who understood the true interests of the people, instead of lordlings and scions of the nobility'.[4]

A meeting at Newhall Hill, in the city centre, on 19 June 1837, demanded only a limited extension of the franchise but by December, when the LWMA had committed itself to the broad democratic principle of the Six Points, Attwood, prompted also by the worsening economic situation, moved towards universal suffrage as a tactical move to broaden the base of the campaign. Within a short time, the Council further refined its strategy, proposing missionary tours to provincial centres, collecting signatures to a National Petition, with each town meeting electing delegates to a future assembly. This new forum would oversee the national campaign and be supported by a 'national rent', funds collected at each mass meeting.

In essence, this was the framework for the National Convention or the 'People's Parliament' which was eventually to be responsible for submitting the petition to Parliament. If it was rejected, then in the view of the Birmingham radicals, the Convention would have the authority to decide on any further measures. At this stage, Birmingham was considering the traditional weapon of the boycott, in particular reducing government revenue by a mass refusal to buy goods subject to excise such as beer - not perhaps a tactic with much promise of success. At times Attwood was to talk of a 'sacred week', a general strike of workers and employers. On one occasion, he declared that 'if our enemies shed blood - if they attack the people - they must take the consequences upon their own heads'.[5]

On 14 May 1838, the BPU published its National Petition aimed at securing further political reform. They decided to open their campaign in Glasgow, where the recent sentence of seven years' transportation passed on five members of a cotton spinners union had angered Glasgow and fellow trade unionists and radicals throughout the country. It was seen as another 'Tolpuddle', and a support committe was immediately established. Glasgow, it was assumed, would need little persuading to join the national crusade launched in the Midlands. Five prominent members of the BPU, including Attwood and Muntz, travelled to Scotland and spoke at a mass meeting on 21 May to explain the purpose of the petition. From the LWMA, Dr Wade and Thomas Murphy outlined the People's Charter. In the history of Chartism this Glasgow meeting is significant not only in marking the alliance of two major pressure groups, and in the mutual acceptance of their separate programmes, but also in bringing the movement firmly onto the national stage.

On 6 August 1838, a mass meeting in Birmingham adopted both the National Petition and the People's Charter. This meeting, writes Mark Hovell, 'is the official beginning of the Chartist Movement, that is of all working-class radicals in one movement'.[6] Henry Hetherington and Henry Vincent from the LWMA linked Birmingham with the London radicals; the presence on the platform of Feargus O'Connor cemented, if only temporarily, a tri-partite pact of BPU, LWMA, and the northern wing of the movement.

5 Feargus O'Connor

By the winter of 1838-9, Feargus O'Connor was beginning to assume the mantle of natural leader of the Chartist Movement, and in working-class eyes, was filling the place once held by Henry Hunt, the gentleman radical and bogeyman of post-1815 governments. By now in his early forties, O'Connor had first come into prominence as a member of Daniel O'Connell's Irish party which the Catholic Emancipation Bill of 1829 had brought into the Commons. He belonged to an Irish Protestant landowning family from County Meath, well-known for its radicalism and support for Irish independence.

In 1832, he was elected to the reformed Parliament as MP for County Cork on a platform of universal suffrage, annual parliaments, and the secret ballot. After his electoral victory, he proved to be a difficult colleague in the House, unable to swallow the party line on Repeal. The Irish party leader, Daniel O'Connell, was prepared to work with the Whigs and shelve Repeal of the Union until the time was ripe. Not so O'Connor. Such a policy, he argued, was abandoning promises he had made to his constitutents. A further cause of friction was his opposition to the Poor Law Amendment Act which Daniel O'Connell supported.

Although in the general election early in 1835 he again won his Cork seat, he was disqualified on a technicality. The death of the great radical journalist MP, William Cobbett, caused a by-election in the summer of 1835 in his Oldham constituency. Although Cobbett's son, John Morgan Cobbett, was standing, he was thought to be uncommitted to disestablishment of the Church of England (at that time a major Nonconformist concern), so O'Connor put himself forward. But the result was that he split the radical vote, thereby allowing the Tory candidate to take the seat.

Denied a return to Parliament, he threw himself once more into London's radical politics. Oldham proved to be a valuable educational experience. There he had forged links which proved to be permanent with its leaders (the other Oldham MP was the radical factory owner John Fielden), and there for the first time he saw 'the dark satanic mills' which were spreading over the northern countryside. Back in London, he spoke at Tolpuddle support meetings and helped to set up the Marylebone Radical Association, the model for similar London-based associations.

From this base, O'Connor set out on a successful tour of the North, which led to the forming of a chain of radical associations in textile towns such as Stockport, Rochdale and Keighley. In the mill towns, he preached the same political message, fundamentally a fore-runner of the Chartist programme. His purpose was to weld together the northern associations into a national organisation which would form the basis for a future National Convention, in essence to create a working-class party.

6 The *Northern Star*

Unlike its radical predecessors such as the *Poor Man's Guardian*, when the *Northern Star* first appeared on 18 November 1837 it bore the

Feargus O'Connor

penny stamp which gave the paper the legal right to report news and to enjoy free postal delivery throughout the country. The proprietor was Feargus O'Connor and its editor the Revd William Hill, a sectarian minister from Hull. O'Connor's plan was to create a national working-class newspaper, based not on London but upon a provincial centre with a strong radical tradition which would serve to keep the paper afloat in its critical early days. Published in Leeds on Saturday morning, it was claimed that it could be bought in London that same evening. Its initial costs were met by a share flotation first in Hull, where Hill had funds available, and then in all the main Yorkshire towns - in Leeds, Halifax, Bradford and Huddersfield.

The time was ripe for such a venture. The Anti-Poor Law campaign was then at its height and the *Northern Star* carried full reports of the fierce local protests and covered the speeches of Stephens, Oastler and, of course, O'Connor himself. The paper also took up the case of the Glasgow cotton spinners and assumed the leadership of what was now a major national campaign. In pursuing new causes, the one great cause was not lost sight of and, through its columns, the *Northern Star* never ceased to remind its readers that the ultimate goal was universal suffrage.

Despite its relatively high price, the new paper established itself very quickly. By Christmas 1837, it was selling around 10,000 copies a week and in the July days of 1839, when the petition was presented to the Commons, its sales peaked at around 50,000. Yet the number of copies sold gives little real indication of how widely the paper was read. The Star could be found in public houses and in clubs; reading societies were set up to sieve and discuss its bulletin of Chartist activities. Again, there are many contemporary accounts of Sunday morning gatherings to hear and savour the message from Leeds.

The *Star* was distributed through local radical booksellers, often those who had sold the unstamped papers such as the *Poor Man's Guardian*. That legendary radical figure, the shoe-maker, appears occasionally as a seller, but more often as a reader to the many who could not read. Sales were expanded by techniques more familiar in the twentieth century when, for instance, the weekly issue would include woodcuts of famous radicals such as William Cobbett and Henry Hunt.

What then was its significance in the Chartist movement? Karl Marx's collaborator, Friedrich Engels, then living in Manchester, commented that the *Star* was 'the only sheet which reports all the movements of the proletariat.'[7] It was a paper for the working class and read only by the working class. It served to give a sense of national purpose and national unity to Chartist supporters scattered throughout the land; it brought to all its readers hope that a new world was about to be born.

7 Chartism in the North

In the northern mill towns, the winter of 1837 witnessed a major campaign, headed by Oastler, O'Connor and the fiery Methodist preacher Joseph Rayner Stephens, directed against the new 'Bastilles', the workhouses designed to house the unemployed and destitute poor. This had culminated in the motion introduced into the Commons in February 1838 by John Fielden for the repeal of the Poor Law Amendment Act. Backed by a nation-wide petition, signed by more than 100,000, it was nevertheless heavily defeated. As a consequence, throughout the North, it was generally resolved to abandon petitioning altogether. Yet the autumn and winter of 1838-9 saw the birth of a petitioning movement far exceeding in mass support any that had gone before.

What new hope, then, inspired the people to make yet another attempt to secure legislative change by a mass petitioning campaign? A partial answer lies in the tactic, deployed by O'Connor, of coupling a demand for the withdrawal of the hated law with the call for universal suffrage, in this way keeping before his audiences what he saw as the essential link between the two reforms. Again, the new campaign built upon an already existing structure. The petition for the Charter was 'taken up by organisations already in existence, propounded by speakers already practised in their craft in the factory, anti-Poor Law and earlier radical movements'.[8] Furthermore, in the eyes of many radicals, the failure of earlier petitions owed much to their being single-issue campaigns. Chartism they saw as a root and branch movement which, by bringing the people as a whole into the political nation, would ensure that their voice would be reflected in the actions of Parliament.

What was new in the campaign was the ominous and insistent claim that this petition would be the last - the implicit question of what would happen if yet again the campaign failed alarmed both government and its post-1832 supporters. The language from the platform often hinted at the need to arm, and LWMA speakers, such as Henry Vincent, in their countrywide tours, noted the determination of Lancashire and Yorkshire radicals to resort to force if this final petition failed.

8 Chartist Rhetoric

To make clear the overwhelming extent of the people's support became the principal tactic adopted by O'Connor and the northern movement. The mass meeting, procession or demonstration was to be the moral force before which the government would finally yield. In this campaign of moral persuasion, the radical press, in particular the *Northern Star*, the voice of O'Connor, was an essential element. Another was Feargus O'Connor himself. Now at the height of his physical and intellectual powers, he toured the country addressing meetings nationwide. In one month, spanning Christmas 1838, he spoke at 22 meetings and covered more than 1,500 miles. He referred to the inevitability of further action should the Charter be rejected but was careful not to say what form this would take.

O'Connor's platform style, at once humorous, passionate and with a persuasive message of hope, won for him a great popular following with working-class audiences. In one vein he would ridicule the hypocrisy of the wealthy aristocracy as in this passage:

> Harry Brougham said they wanted no poor law as every young man ought to lay up a provision for old age, yet while he said this with one side of his mouth, he was screwing the other side to get his retiring pension raised from £4,000 to £5,000 a year.

In another, when the Great Northern Union was in the making, he told his audiences:

> London, Birmingham, Sheffield, Manchester, Leeds, Newcastle, Carlisle, Glasgow and Edinburgh, had now become forged as it were together … a spirit was now growing which nothing but justice could put down.

And later in this same tour in 1838, he spelled out his political creed:

> I say again, first get universal suffrage, and don't be putting the cart before the horse, then when the reins are in your hands, you will be enabled to guide the chariot of the State in peace and safety.[9]

The two most influential platform speakers of the winter campaign other than O'Connor were John Fielden and Joseph Rayner Stephens. Although O'Connor and Stephens often spoke at the same meetings, in emphasis and tone they differed profoundly. While O'Connor campaigned on a political platform, Stephens, a Methodist preacher and veteran of the factory and anti-Poor Law campaigns, returned continually to his favourite themes, the social evils of factory and 'Bastille.' What finally decided the government to arrest him was his call at a Kersal Moor meeting for a 'war to the knife' with a threat that 'the palace shall be in flames' - this at a time when torchlight meetings were a new and alarming type of demonstration. The violence of his rhetoric, focusing on the Poor Law Commission, and the wide-ranging nature of his threats, can be be judged by this extract from that speech. It draws also on the fundamental radical interpretation of the source of wealth.

1   If this damnable law, which violated all the laws of God, was continued, and all the means of peaceably putting an end to it had been made in vain, then in the words of their banner, 'For children and wife we'll war to the knife'. If the people who produce all wealth could not be allowed
5   the kindly fruits of the earth which they had raised by the sweat of their brow, then war to the knife with their enemies, who were the enemies

of God. If the musket and the pistol, the sword and the pike were of no avail, let the women take the scissors, the child the pin or needle. If all failed, then the firebrand - aye the firebrand - the firebrand I repeat. The 10 palace shall be in flames, if the cottage is not permitted to be the abode of man and wife, and if the smiling infant is to be dragged from a father's arms and a mother's bosom, it is because these hell-hounds of commissioners have set up the command of their master the devil, against our God.[10]

John Fielden, MP for Oldham, who had also been active in the Factory and Poor Law campaigns, was a millionaire industrialist, the owner of a Todmorden factory employing more than 3,000 workers. His political mentor was Thomas Jefferson, a founding father of the American Republic, and his address to the crowd at that same Kersal Moor meeting included a lengthy quotation from Jefferson which declared :

1 that all men are created equal, that they are endowed by their creator with certain unalienable Rights, that among these are Life, Liberty and the Pursuit of Happiness - That to secure these rights, Governments are instituted amongst Men, deriving their just powers from the consent of 5 the governed - That whenever any Form of Government become destructive of these ends, it is the Right of the People to alter or to abolish it.[11]

For Fielden, the Chartist demands fell clearly within the political tradition of the American Revolution, and were based upon a just claim to popular sovereignty from those who suffered the burden of taxation without representation. Where he increasingly differed with his fellow Chartists was on the length to which political intimidation, the rhetoric of violence, should be allowed to go.

These mass meetings had two distinct purposes: the traditional function of collecting signatures for the National Petition and the new responsibility of electing delegates to the National Convention which was to present the Chartist petition to Parliament. Many Chartists, however, saw the Convention as leading inevitably to a 'People's Parliament', a genuinely democratic alternative to the existing unrepresentative House of Commons.

9 The Great Northern Union

Of the three main organisations working in the autumn and winter campaign of 1838-9, the Great Northern Union (GNU), the voice of the workers in the mill towns, commanded the most support. The balance had clearly tilted towards the O'Connorites and relations with the LWMA and BPU had become increasingly tense. The belligerent tone of the northern movement had alienated the artisan radicals of the LWMA, and in turn O'Connor and the northern Chartists found intolerable the LWMA's close association with Daniel O'Connell, the scourge of trade unions. With the BPU, at this stage, however, tactics were not an issue. Indeed one member of the Political Council, the ruling elite of the BPU, had commented that 'the terrors of a few Newhall Hill meetings would induce them [the government] to relax the screw'.[12] What was at issue between O'Connor and Attwood was the question of the ultimate control of the movement, given the mass following of the one and the assumed natural right to leadership of the other. Within the BPU, too, cracks began to appear as the rank and file began to question its oligarchic nature. The BPU was very much top-heavy. Of the eight delegates elected to the proposed Convention, seven belonged to Birmingham's mercantile or industrialist class. Its elitist nature was rapidly becoming a general source of resentment to working-class supporters.

The GNU, essentially a loose federation of radical associations, had its political heartland in West Yorkshire where O'Connor's support was at its strongest. It was formally established at a meeting on 5 June 1838 on Hunslet Moor, near Leeds. One of its articles carried a clear commitment to the use of physical force if moral force should fail, a commitment which came to be summed up in the phrase, 'peaceably if we may, forcibly if we must', the slogan printed on the membership cards of the LDA.

The winter campaigns of 1838-9 in the northern manufacturing districts encouraged the sense that change, fundamental change, was inevitable. The mass meetings themselves followed the model of that historic meeting on 16 August 1819 at St Peter's Fields, Manchester, as workers and families, dressed in their Sunday best, assembling in Yorkshire at Peep Green or in Lancashire on Kersal Moor, moved in orderly procession with brass bands playing and banners and flags flying to listen to the speeches from the platform. The fear, also, was that the subsequent repression, the massacre of 'Peterloo', still strong in popular memory, would be re-enacted by the army. But the government behaved with commendable restraint, and although the language of the platform was charged with emotion and laced with references to 'dying as freemen rather than living like slaves', crowd behaviour was always exemplary.

Stephens and O'Connor decided on a new tactic of shifting demonstrations from the moors to the centre of the manufacturing towns, which seemed to pose a direct threat to property and public order. It began first on 2 October in Stockport, where a crowd of Chartist supporters, meeting in the market square and armed with torches, proceeded to the town's factory district. In November 1838, O'Connor, speaking at a Rochdale meeting, was fairly specific about the consequences which rejection of the Charter would entail, citing a deadline of 29 September 1839 for its acceptance:

ı If the Whigs did not concede their liberty on the 29th, the people should

take it by force on the 30th. He had preached peace all his life, but at
the same time he was always prepared for war. One of those torches
(pointing at one near at hand) was worth a thousand speeches: it spoke
5 a language so intelligible that no-one could misunderstand.[13]

In December, understandably fearful of possible arson attacks, the
government arrested Stephens and banned torchlight processions.
Nevertheless, O'Connor, with what seemed unnecessary bravado,
challenged this ban by addressing a further torchlight meeting, once
more re-iterating that force might be necessary:

1 By reference to my speeches and writing it will be found that I have
never so much as said 'arm'. But now I say 'arm', and I having said it, the
fulfillment shall rest with the whole people. 'Arm'; but in nowise use
those arms - offensively nor defensively as individuals...They must in
5 nowise be used against the constitution even in your united strength'.[14]

Paradoxically, O'Connor, concerned that riots, possibly inspired by
government agents, should not put at risk his political objective of a
National Convention, then called upon his supporters to abandon
torchlight meetings. He followed this up in the *Northern Star* by
emphasising to his fellow Chartists that their collective purpose was
not social but political, the vote, not the repeal of the Poor Law
Amendment Act. In this, O'Connor was not denying the urgency of
the need to repeal the hated Poor Law but rather trying to establish
his priorities: that the fundamental purpose of Chartism was to
achieve political citizenship for its supporters.

10 The Chartist National Convention

The Chartist Convention first met on 4 February 1839, at the British
Hotel, Cockspur Street, in London, and then moved to more permanent quarters in Bolt Court, Fleet Street. Its title asserted the
Convention's claim to be seen within that tradition established by the
American and French Revolutions. Similar high hopes, too, were
riding on this assembly, for many Chartists saw the Convention, whose
members were directly elected at mass meetings, as more representative than a House of Commons elected on its property-based franchise. Its revolutionary pretensions were summed up by O'Connor in
his claim that 'it was the only constituted authority representing the
people of this country'.[15] In common, too, with its revolutionary
forbears, its members in the artist's sketch of the 'General
Convention of the Industrious Classes' (see page 39) look uncompro-
misingly middle-class.

Of the 53 elected members, rather fewer than half were working-
class. Even with financial assistance from the 'National Rent', the
collections made at Chartist meetings, working-class men were reluctant to run the risk of losing their jobs in their absence at the

The Convention

Convention. The largest group came from the industrial North, 20 in all, a mix of different trades and professions, a journalist, a tea dealer, a shoe-maker amongst them. The BPU elected seven members, of whom only four arrived, including John Collins, its sole working-class delegate. The LWMA sent William Lovett and seven other delegates.

The Convention moved first to elect a secretary and, despite some protests from the floor that he was out of touch with feelings in the North, William Lovett was chosen. The Convention then tried to work out a strategy should the House of Commons reject the petition. Feargus O'Connor, who not only commanded most support in the Convention but had the ability to carry delegates with him, proposed in these words that they should prepare for 'ulterior measures'.

> 1 The best way to make an impression upon them was to go with the petition in one hand and the ulterior measures in the other. If anything could give increased energy to the people it would be the knowledge of the fact, that as soon as the petition was rejected…the Convention would
> 5 do something, within the law, which would afford a demonstration of the people's strength and determination.[16]

O'Connnor's language was deliberately cautious, yet the suggestion that Chartism should go beyond peaceful petitioning triggered off the first crisis and the first resignation. One of Cobbett's sons, J.P. Cobbett, a Manchester delegate, moved a resolution calling on the Convention to limit itself to presenting the petition. When this was defeated, he resigned.

Although London was a convenient place to meet and meeting in the capital gave additional prestige to a body which made such grand claims, London's radical credentials were essentially moderate, mirrored in the LWMA. Spitalfields, home to the silk weavers, was an exception. This district was the stronghold of the London Democratic Association, led by the delegate George Julian Harney. Within the Convention, Harney quickly emerged as a committed advocate of revolutionary tactics. In a speech to Derby Chartists in January, which ended by the meeting electing him as their representative to the Convention, he had vividly evoked the aftermath of the failure of the petitioning movement:

> 1 Universal Suffrage there shall be - or - our tyrants will find to their cost that we will have universal misery … We will make our country one vast, howling wilderness of desolation and destruction rather than the tyrants shall carry out their infernal system. I have given you to under-
> 5 stand that the men of the North are armed. I invite you to follow their example … Believe me, there is no argument like the sword - and the musket is unanswerable.[17]

The increasingly militant tone of the debates antagonised some delegates, many of whom simply drifted away and returned home. With the exception of John Collins, all the BPU delegates left. The decision of the BPU delegates to leave is at first difficult to reconcile with their original commitment to 'ulterior measures' and Attwood's occasional threats of force. Yet to the Birmingham middle class, there may have come some realisation of where their continuing support might lead. Within a very short time the Convention had shrunk to half of its original strength. As a way of renewing grass-roots support, O'Connor proposed that the Convention should become peripatetic, moving round provincial centres in turn. Another strong reason for leaving London was the growing fear that government would soon move against them either as individuals or as a body. It was known that mail was being opened and spies were assumed to be in every public meeting. Suspicion even centred on delegates themselves. Revolutionaries such as Harney were thought by some moderates to be paid government agents, planted amongst them to incite them to treasonable acts which would justify government reprisals!

When in May 1839 the Whig government of Lord Melbourne resigned, the Convention took the final decision to move to Birmingham, now a militant Chartist centre. There was a general fear amongst delegates that if the forthcoming election led to the return of a hard-line Tory government, they would be in immediate danger in London. Even at this juncture, the delegates were divided amongst themselves. Two important propositions hung on this decision. O'Connor had linked the move with the necessity to hammer out in Birmingham the intended 'ulterior measures ' and had taken the provocative step of defining the Convention as 'the only constitutional representative of the people'. Although moderates at first refused to agree with either proposition, ultimately they were carried along by the threatened prospect of another Tory government.

11 The Convention in Birmingham

On 7 May the Convention left London and, re-inforced by mainly working-class replacements, 35 delegates re-assembled in Birmingham six days later. Its first task was to define what form ulterior measures should take. A provisional list was drawn up which it was proposed should be submitted to mass meetings held over the coming Whitsun weekend. They ranged from the familiar tactic of withdrawing funds from banks to exclusive dealing - that is a boycott of anti-Chartist traders. Where they moved into new territory was in calling for a 'sacred month' and for the arming of Chartist supporters. Many delegates considered the 'sacred month' or general strike as a non-violent measure consonant with a policy of moral force, despite Harney's warning that within a week starving workers would be foraging for food and violent clashes would inevitably follow. The Convention's call to arms in a society where the right to bear arms was still sanctioned was generally accepted as a necessary precaution against an unprovoked attack by government forces.

In London, O'Connor had tried to hold the balance between moderates and militants. His strategy was similar to that deployed by the BPU in the 'Days of May' of the Reform Bill crisis (see pages 12-14): confrontation not revolution. There must, he insisted, be no misunderstanding: this was the last petition; the patience of the people was running out and rejection would lead inevitably to 'ulterior measures'. O'Connor remained convinced that the petition, backed up by mass meetings, with the implicit menace of possible further action, would bring the authorities to heel. However, J. Epstein points out that when the Convention adjourned until 1 July, no clear priority had been established regarding the list of ulterior measures 'and the decision to leave this matter to the will of the simultaneous meetings represented an abnegation of the Convention's leadership responsibilities'.[18]

Before the Convention adjourned, Henry Vincent, a prominent Chartist lecturer, had been arrested, as had two other delegates. Tempers were rising and rioting had broken out in several parts of the country. In the North, Chartists had been arrested for drilling. Faced by a growing threat to public order, the government responded by a ban on drilling and placing new restrictions on public meetings. Anticipating a wave of arrests, the Chartists made plans for alternative representatives and O'Connor set up a National Defence Fund. The planned mass meetings went ahead with the clear intention of making a show of strength: to display the collective force of the Chartist movement. The impact was lessened by their taking place not simultaneously but on different days in May, albeit fairly close together. The meeting at Kersal Moor on 25 May was perhaps typical of them all, attended, as a Home Office report shows, by families in holiday mood, akin perhaps to a fete or open-air theatre. At a meeting in Leeds, O'Connor broached a new idea: that the people must constitute an army 'not of offence, but of reserve' ready to strike back in the case of attack. That response should take the form of arson attacks - the unspecified targets being, no doubt, the local cotton and woollen mills. Many Chartists were convinced that, given an attack by workers on a mill, the rank and file of the army, coming from the same social background as the attackers, would hold their fire and perhaps even fraternise with the crowd. Neither O'Connor nor the officer in charge, General Sir Charles James Napier, himself sympathetic to the Chartists, shared this opinion. Both were convinced that, in any confrontation between the Army and a hostile crowd, the soldiers would obey the commands of their officers.

In these critical weeks, there was little uniformity in the advice of the Chartist spokesmen. On the left, Harney was advancing a theory of the 'sacred right of insurrection', while O'Connor's paper, the *Star*, was advising its readers to go unarmed to meetings so as to avoid provocation. With Peterloo still in mind, this cautionary advice found a mainly responsive audience. However, both people and government were convinced that conflict was increasingly likely, given the truculence on one side and the intransigence on the other.

When in July the Convention re-assembled, they immediately debated the ulterior measures they would recommend if the petition - due to be submitted on 12 July - should be rejected. Acutely aware that to fix on the sacred month would be tantamount to accepting the inevitability of clashes between workers and the Army, the Convention decided that they would meet on the day after Parliament had debated the petition, on July 13, to decide, if need be, on a starting date for the sacred month. Despite calls for caution, the Convention had moved significantly closer to revolutionary confrontation.

Although in the debates O'Connor had argued for the sacred month, he now sought to suggest the outlines of a different strategy. He had become convinced that the propertied classes could easily sit out a general strike and that the only sufferers would be the strikers themselves. Although no advocate of revolution, he talked of a defensive uprising, prompted by the action of government, such as the arrest of the Convention or a Peterloo-style attack upon a peaceful assembly. At meetings across the country, he spoke openly of the need to be armed, to be vigilant, and ready to offer justified resistance to tyranny.

12 The Bull Ring Riots

The testing time came earlier than expected. On 4 July, Convention members and local Chartists held a meeting in the Bull Ring, Birmingham's traditional forum, the scene of many BPU meetings during the Reform Bill agitation. In early May, Chartist meetings had become a daily occurrence, drawing largely working-class crowds, and were a source of irritation to local business men. Shopkeepers complained that these meetings were affecting their trade. As a consequence, the Birmingham magistrates, three of whom were ex-political councillors of the BPU, banned any further meetings. Although the gathering on 4 July was wholly peaceful, with women and children amongst the crowd, the mayor, William Scholefield, himself an ex-member of the BPU's Political Council, decided to call in the hated Metropolitan police.

With the mayor in the lead, the London police, 60 in all, lightly armed with staffs, set about trying to disperse the meeting, estimated as around 1,000, and to arrest the speakers. After momentary panic, the crowd rallied and turned upon the police, of whom two were only saved from certain death by the intervention of Dr John Taylor, a Convention delegate. The army were then brought in and, under their protection, the police were successful in making some arrests. During the night, Dr John Taylor was also arrested. The next day the Convention condemned the authorities' actions in a series of resolutions and then posted copies, signed by William Lovett as secretary, on the walls of the city. The Birmingham magistrates responded swiftly by arresting Lovett, together with John Collins, who had been responsible for printing the resolutions.

Although the Bull Ring affair superficially resembles 'Peterloo', the differences are perhaps more significant. In Birmingham there were no sabres being wielded on a defenceless crowd, only wooden staffs. As a consequence no lives were lost. Twenty years after Peterloo, local JPs were no longer willing to use armed force to break up a political meeting. However, the Army was involved, albeit in a supportive role, and no fraternisation between soldiers and working-class Chartists took place - as O'Connor was quick to point out. Yet despite the obvious differences between 'Peterloo' and the Bull Ring Riots, the action of the Birmingham magistrates exhibits the same lack of judgement as that of their fellows in Manchester in mounting so unprovoked an attack, particularly at a time when militant Chartists were prepared to see such an attack as justifying an uprising.

The Birmingham arrests triggered off a series of protest meetings, in the end to no avail. In August, Lovett and Collins were each sentenced to 12 months imprisonment, a much lighter sentence than some members of the jury, who had openly expressed their conviction that all Chartists should be hanged, had hoped for. At the same assizes, three other Chartists were condemned to death for their part in the Bull Ring riots, although later the sentences were commuted to transportation for life. Dr John Taylor, one of the most fervent advocates of physical force, rivalled perhaps only by Julian Harney, was like Harney himself never brought to trial.

13 The Chartist Petition in the House of Commons

The Chartist petition was submitted to the House of Commons on 12 July, with 1,280,000 signatures. Attwood and Fielden sponsored a motion that a committee of the whole House should consider the petition. Their proposal hinged on a traditional Parliamentary procedure which would allow MPs ample time to discuss the merits of the Chartist case. In moving the motion, Attwood made a low-key speech, hardly touching on his favourite theme, currency reform, but concentrating on economic conditions, leaving aside entirely the Chartist demand for equal civil and political rights. Furthermore he implicitly anticipated defeat by arguing for more modest constitutional reform: household suffrage, for instance, rather than universal suffrage.

The House was in no mood for prolonged discussion - the summer recess drew near - but Benjamin Disraeli, the rising star of the Tory party, while not supporting the motion, offered an analysis of present discontents, blaming them on the failure of the middle class to exercise those great social duties which had been the hallmark of the ancient aristocracy. In the pre-1832 past, he suggested, the minority that possessed political rights also guarded the civil rights of the great majority, and had acted with consistent benevolence towards the rest of society. The new political masters, the middle class, had failed to follow in that tradition as the passing of the Poor Law Amendment Act clearly showed, so while he could not approve of the Charter, he sympathised with the Chartists.

On a vote, the House rejected the petition by 235 votes to 46. Two days after this defeat, the two MPs met with Convention representatives and recommended that the next step should be to organise a separate petition from every parish in the kingdom, rather than a single mass petition. The Chartist delegates were opposed to any further petitioning and said that they intended to go ahead with the 'sacred month' - a month-long general strike. After this defeat, Attwood fell away; Fielden remained committed to universal suffrage for the rest of his life but parted company with Chartists on this question of tactics.

The Convention, now reduced to 24 members, then debated whether to fix a date for a general strike but O'Connor persuaded the delegates not to go down that road. The final debates revealed how deep the divisions were within the leadership. Both Dr John Taylor and Harney were pressing for action which would lead inevitably to an armed uprising. O'Connor was acutely aware of how disastrous the outcome could be with a poorly armed and poorly led crowd facing a well equipped and highly trained fighting force. He was now looking to a future where the Movement could re-group and would be controlled by a permanent body and, despite the accusations of cowardice bandied about in the Convention, he stood firm against any policy which would lead to an armed rising.

14 The Newport Rising

On the morning of 4 November 1839, a column of 7,000 Chartists, many armed with pikes or muskets, advanced into the small Monmouthshire town of Newport and within minutes were met with concentrated rifle fire which left at least 22 of them dead or dying. During most of their long overnight march there had been torrential rain and only fanatical determination, it might seem, could have driven these exhausted, rain-soaked men into so desperate an action. Since then, historians have raked over the evidence of the Rising to try to make some sense of what took place. Was it perhaps a mass demonstration that went tragically wrong? Was it the work of *agents provocateurs*? Was Newport intended to be the signal for a general uprising - which never took place? Many of these questions are still without a clear answer as, after its failure, Chartists in Wales closed ranks and their secrets died with them.

One answer to the question 'why South Wales rather than

Yorkshire?' is provided by David Jones in his analysis of the social and economic geography of the area. He quotes from Thomas Phillips, Mayor of Newport and defender of the Westgate hotel where the attack took place. Some years after the Rising, Phillips advanced the view that 'Chartism is found in all its worst manifestations - not as an adhesion to political dogmas, but as an indication of that class antagonism … which originated, as great social evils ever do, in the neglect of duty by the master, the ruling class'.[19] This contemporary indictment chimes in with Disraeli's analysis of the embittered class relations which he had seen as the root cause of the Chartist movement. 'Duty' conjures up the seigneurial relationship which the Welsh plutocracy aped but in the Welsh valleys it was singularly lacking that benovolence Disraeli had identified as a necessary social cement.

Iron production was dominated by Anglican non-Welsh speaking iron-masters such as the Homfrays of Tredegar, whose mansion was fortified with guns and cannon. They behaved like lords of the manor towards a native population who shared neither their language nor their creed. Religion was a major divisive force. The Anglican church had little importance in the lives of working people. In the mining and iron villages and towns, Nonconformist chapels of every kind - Baptist, Independent, Primitive and Wesleyan Methodist - offered faith and fellowship. Unlike iron-masters, mine-owners were usually non-resident and left day-to-day control in the hands of their local agents who were often less anglicised than the owners. What both mine agents and iron-masters had in common was the formal and informal network of social and economic control over their workforce. It was they who owned shops and public houses and workers' homes. As JPs and Poor Law Guardians, they were also responsible for carrying out the minimal state obligations of the day.

Early nineteenth-century Welsh working-class society was built upon a series of interlocking relationships. In the claustrophobic, disease-ridden villages, strong ties bonded local families together, in part a reflection of the forced inter-dependence of the workplace itself. In the bad times, neighbour would help neighbour. Another offshoot was the almost spontaneous appearance of combinations, early forms of trade unions, when the need arose. Men formed trade societies to fight savage wage cuts or to challenge the abuses of the truck system, the practice by which companies owned the local shop, selling food and beer, and providing credit. In the events of 3-4 November, this strong sense of community impelled men to join their workmates and neighbours, either from a sense of moral obligation or from group loyalty.

In this tightly-knit society, Chartism took ready root. In 1838, a Working Men's Association (WMA) was founded in Newport, a rapidly expanding commercial centre, connected by rail, river and canal to the rest of the country. From Newport, 'missionaries' were posted to the neighbouring towns where sister associations were readily established. At first, like the LWMA on which these WMAs were modelled, members were mainly artisan with a scattering of local tradesmen, butchers, grocers, shoe-makers and publicans. By the spring of 1839, however, colliers were flooding in and signing the Chartist petition. In his missionary tours in South Wales, Henry Vincent, emissary of the LWMA, recruited large numbers of workers in the mines and in the foundries. Newport's growing importance as a Chartist centre was reflected in the election of John Frost, a local draper and JP, as its delegate to the National Convention.

The failure of the petition, followed by the Convention's abandonment of the sacred month, prompted the more militant of the Welsh Chartists to turn to alternative ways to make the Charter a reality. Their resolution was strengthened by a series of repressive steps taken by the authorities. The much-loved Henry Vincent was arrested; warnings were issued against the radical press; publicans known to be sympathetic to Chartism were refused licences. Yet despite these precautionary measures, no move was made to increase the army presence in the area.

By September 1839, local leaders had fixed a date for a march on Newport, and a command structure, based upon active cells of ten, was partially in place. What the overall plan was, is still not quite clear. Henry Vincent was held in degrading circumstances in Monmouth gaol - and his release was thought to be one major objective, although Monmouth is many miles from Newport. The view that it was intended to be no more than a mass demonstration does not readily account for the extent of armed preparation or, for that matter, the widely-held conviction amongst local Chartists that, in the victorious aftermath, hated class enemies would be taken hostage and held captive in coal-pits. Again, some Chartists expected that, after the fall of Newport, attacks would then be launched against other South Wales towns. In turn, this would trigger off movements throughout the country which would force the government to yield. Dorothy Thompson, in assessing this expectation, writes: 'The successful occcupation of a provincial town was probably intended to act as an inspiration for similar acts in other parts of the country, rather than to form the first of a series of inter-connected risings which had already been planned'.[20] The capture of Newport, others thought, would be achieved without injury on either side, as soldiers would not fire on their working-class brethren. However, the driving force, as David Jones stresses, 'was to obtain the political rights which were denied them'.[21]

On Sunday night, 3 November, the march on Newport began. Men converged on the town from many different Welsh communities, some coming from as far away as Ebbw Vale, on the way picking up others, either by persuasion or by intimidation (see map on page 49). John Frost, the delegate for Newport, was universally accepted as their leader. Some marchers were armed with home-made pikes or guns but many with nothing at all. There had been scarcely any prior briefing of the marchers as to how their action would achieve their purpose of securing the Charter, so that many who entered Newport that morning were risking their lives in ignorance of their leaders' intentions.

At about 9 o'clock on the morning of 4 November, the marchers reached Newport. In the front, the column was moving with military precision, flanked by men bearing arms. They continued to the Westgate hotel where some local Chartists, taken during the night, were held by the mayor and special constables. It is unlikely that the Chartists knew that this volunteer force had now been strengthened by 32 soldiers of the 45th Regiment who had taken up defensive positions there. No-one knows who fired the first shot but, after the first exchange, the Chartists forced their way into the hotel where the steady fire from the soldiers killed many of those who had got inside. One who died there was George Shell, an 18 year old from Pontypool who left a brief note of explanation to his parents. It ran:

> I shall this night be engaged in a glorious struggle for freedom, and should it please God to spare my life, I shall see you soon; but if not, grieve not for me, I shall have fallen in a noble cause.[22]

In the mass trial which followed, 21 Welsh Chartists were charged with high treason and John Frost and two others were sentenced to the barbaric death prescribed by law. However, the presiding judge, Chief Justice Tindal, had added a very strong recommendation for mercy, and after the trial, he continued to press this advice directly on government ministers. In the end, he prevailed and the three leaders' sentences were commuted to transportation. Five other defendants were also sentenced to a similar exile. The remaining 13 prisoners were treated fairly leniently with sentences of up to a year's imprisonment.

15 Conclusion

The trial of Frost and his fellow Chartists in Monmouth and their subsequent sentences evoked nation-wide massive protest meetings, and a simultaneous petitioning campaign to try to save their lives. At the same time, throughout January 1840, violent confrontations took place between the authorities and Chartists in several Yorkshire towns, in Bradford, Dewsbury and Sheffield, with reports to the Home Office of plans for a general rising. However the government's wise decision at the end of the month to commute their sentences calmed the country.

By the spring of 1840, Chartism seemed a spent force. Most of the national leaders were imprisoned. O'Connor had been sentenced to 18 months; similar sentences had been passed on O'Brien and Stephens. Vincent, whose detention had so inflamed tempers in

South Wales, was sent to prison for 12 months. Lovett was already serving a 12 month sentence. Throughout the country, active Chartists were brought before the courts, and more than 500 were given sentences ranging from a few weeks to transportation.

The Chartist movement's bid to bring the working class within the political nation had clearly failed. In their attempt, the Chartists had brought the country to the brink of revolution, but in the end they drew back. A minority, drawing on the French experiences of 1789 and 1830, when a Paris crowd toppled a dynasty, had thought that such a revolution could be made in Britain. But London was not Paris and the majority of Chartists were still committed to the legal path to universal suffrage. The attack on Newport did not lead to or provoke similar political turbulence elsewhere. Harney, writing to Engels in

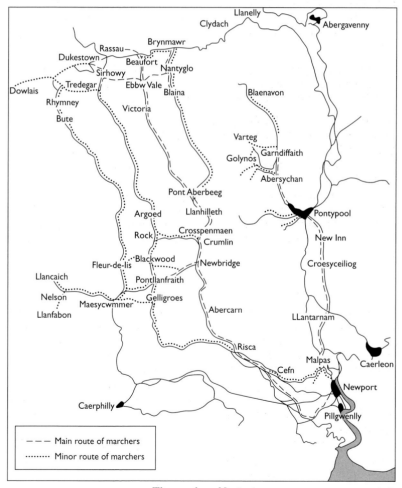

The march on Newport

the 1840s, summed up his assessment of the national mood and Britain's unwillingness to take to the streets:

1   They applaud it at public meetings, but that is all. Notwithstanding all the talk in 1839 about 'arming', the people did not arm and they will not arm … I do not suppose the great changes that will come in this country will come altogether without violence, but combats such as we may look for
5   in France, Germany, Italy and Spain cannot take place in this country.[23]

However, the struggle for the Charter left its mark on governing class and working class alike. To the natural rulers, the Chartist movement seemed to spring out of thin air, already equipped with a set of revolutionary demands - yet, as the evidence shows, the main proposals had been a commonplace of working-class radicalism for many years and had been hammered into a programme during the Reform Bill crisis. So much so that when the Charter was first published it went unremarked in the *Northern Star* simply because it offered nothing new. To the working class, there were the obvious achievements of petition, press and the Convention itself. As J. Epstein observes, the Convention remains as 'a most outstanding example of the potential of the working class to generate alternative political institutions within early capitalist society'.[24]

Again, the rhetoric of violence employed by some Chartists seemed to pose an immediate threat, if not to life, at least to property, but did it differ - except in class origins - from the language of the BPU in 1832? After all, the politics of confrontation, decked out with a call to arms, had been the weapon of the Birmingham middle-class elites in the Reform Bill agitation. Were the Chartists simply marching in the steps of their middle-class predecessors?

A facile comparison is often made between Lovett and O'Connor, as if in themselves they represent fundamentally opposed wings of Chartism: to equate Lovett with moral force and O'Connor with physical force. Does this not ignore Lovett's own commitment, in common with other London radicals, to the use of physical force as a defensive power held in reserve in case of attack? Was O'Connor's attitude fundamentally the same, the difference between the two more a question of personality and ability?

In Chartism, three widely differing regions, the North, the Midlands and London, were temporarily fused into one. All shared a common aim and a common strategy, from the working-class Northern Union through the prosperous Birmingham middle class to the London artisans. In the implicit struggle for power, the GNU had the advantage of its massive popular base. As the Convention deliberated, Birmingham's enthusiasm waned and their delegates withdrew. Lovett and the LWMA, however, persisted in their support. A minority apart, no-one wanted an uprising, so the discussion increasingly turned on the next step, if the petition was rejected. Tried and traditional tactics were discussed, the most familiar being, the boycott and the refusal to buy goods subject to tax. The most potentially dangerous proposal was the 'sacred month' or general strike, a tactic made possible by the speed and extent of industrialisation. Did O'Connor raise expectations - and the temperature - too high in these discussions? And was his unwillingness finally to go down this path a victory for commonsense?

The Convention assembled, deliberated, and then dispersed without any clear gain. In this sense, it was a failure. From the outset, its role was unclear: was it, as some delegates claimed, the People's Parliament, genuinely representative in a way that the House of Commons could never be? If it asserted this claim too vociferously, would this not lead to a dangerous confrontation with the established authorities? Was it perhaps politic to play down this interpretation and to concentrate, as it finally did, on seeing the Petition placed before Parliament? When the Commons refused to consider the Petition, was not the next step, as O'Connor argued, the creation of a central organisation which could plan and supervise any future course of action, an idea which was to be realised by the formation in 1840 of the National Charter Association (see pages 69-70)?

References

1   I.J. Prothero, *Artisans and Politics in Early Nineteenth Century London* (Dawson, 1979), p. 289.
2   Ibid, p. 323.
3   Clive Behagg, *Politics and Production in the Early Nineteenth Century* (Routledge, 1990), p. 196.
4   Clive Behagg, 'An Alliance with the Middle-Class: the Birmingham Political Unions and Early Chartism' in *The Chartist Experience: Studies in Working-Class radicalism and Culture, 1830-60* edited by James Epstein and Dorothy Thompson (Macmillan, 1982), p. 74.
5   Behagg, *The Birmingham Political Union*, p. 76.
6   Mark Hovell, *The Chartist Movement* (Manchester University Press, 1918), p. 107.
7   Ibid, p. 78.
8   Dorothy Thompson, *The Chartists* (Temple Smith, 1984), p. 61.
9   James Epstein, *The Lion of Freedom: Feargus O'Connor and the Chartist Movement, 1832-1842* (Croom Helm, 1982), pp. 112, 106, 107.
10 Joe Finn, *Chartists and Chartism* (Hodder and Stoughton, 1992), pp. 82-3.
11 Stewart Angas Weaver, *John Fielden and the Politics of Popular Radicalism 1832-1847* (Oxford University Press, 1987), p. 198.
12 Behagg, *Politics and Production*, p. 198.
13 Epstein, *The Lion*, p. 120.
14 Ibid, p. 123.
15 Ibid, p. 139.
16 Ibid, p. 149.
17 A.R. Schoyen, *The Chartist Challenge: A Portrait of George Julian Harney* (Heinemann, 1958), p. 49.

18 Epstein, *The Lion*, p. 158.
19 David J.V. Jones, *The Last Rising: The Newport Insurrection of 1839* (Oxford University Press, 1985), p. 25.
20 Thompson, *The Chartists*, p. 85.
21 Jones, *The Last Rising*, p. 208.
22 R.G. Gammage, *History of the Chartist Movement 1837-1854* (1854), second edition 1894, reprinted with an introduction by J. Saville (Frank Cass, 1969), p. 163.
23 Jennifer Bennett, 'The London Democratic Association 1837-41: A Study in London Radicalism' in *The Chartist Experience* ed. Epstein and Thompson, pp. 96-7.
24 Epstein, *The Lion*, p. 186.

Answering source-based questions on 'The Chartist Movement in 1839'

1. *Chartist Rhetoric*

Read the three extracts on pages 38 and 40.

a) Define briefly the following references:
   i) 'the Convention' (line 16 on page 40), (2 marks)
   ii) 'against the constitution' (line 14 on page 38). (2 marks)
b) How far do these extracts present conflicting views of what the next step should be if the 1839 Petition was rejected? (6 marks)
c) Assess the value to the historian of these extracts as representative of the mood of the Convention. (7 marks)
d) On the evidence of these extracts and from your own knowledge, did the British government have good reason to take repressive action against the Chartists? (8 marks)

Bear in mind that the apportionment of marks to each sub-section is an indication of how long or how short an answer should be. If the question is only awarded 2 marks, there is nothing to be gained by a lengthy answer when a single developed point is all that is required.

For instance, in answering a) i), all that is needed is to define what the Convention was and expand that a little by perhaps explaining how the Convention was elected. In answering a) ii) the phrase used by O'Connor should be interpreted in the light of the whole extract from O'Connor's speech. O'Connor is suggesting that the use of arms would be illegal ('against the constitution') if undertaken by an individual but constitutional if 'the whole people' have sanctioned their use.

The second question requires a careful analysis of the three extracts to see where (if at all) they differ. It might be best to start by examining the two statements by O'Connor, sketching in his reputation for brinkmanship and confrontational politicking, and then to consider the threats ('arm' and 'ulterior measures') in both while at the same time showing that he scrupulously insists on the need to act within the law. Again, it might be useful to contrast O'Connor with Harney. You could, if you wished, establish Harney's early reputation as a revolutionary in the French mould and the disturbing effect such declamations had on moderate delegates. It might be worth asking if these were more than empty threats, commenting perhaps on the difficulty of starting to carry them out given the strength of General Napier's forces in the North. Bear in mind that if you are asked 'how far' you are required to make a judgement and bring out any similarities such as the general agreement that there must be a next step if the Petition fails. A simple assertion such as 'not very much' is not enough. Any assertion must be justified.

In considering the third question, it is worthwhile asking if the call for 'ulterior measures' represented the mood of the Convention. Were any 'ulterior measures' actually ever put in place? Is the withdrawal of Cobbett's son and most of the Birmingham delegation a sign of how irresolute - or unconvinced - the Convention as a whole actually were. And didn't Harney himself come under suspicion from the other delegates as a government spy because his rhetoric was so out of tune with the general mood of the Convention?

Question d) gives you an opportunity to develop your own views on the threat that Chartism posed for the authorities. Remember that there is no single right answer to this question. However, any answer must make reference to the extracts as well as your own knowledge. If you judge it relevant, you could, for instance, refer to the Newport Rising or the Bull Ring riots to justify the government's actions, or alternatively to the general orderliness of Chartist behaviour to criticise the wave of arrests.

2. The Next Step
Read the three extracts on pages 35 and 36.
a) Define briefly the following references:
    i) 'hellhounds of commissioners' (lines 6-7 on page 36).
    (2 marks)
    ii) 'unalienable rights' (line 17 on page 36). (2 marks)
b) To what extent do the first and third extracts share similar views on the purpose of universal suffrage? (6 marks)
c) Assess the value to the historian of these three extracts as a guide to the Chartist agitation. (7 marks)
d) 'The Chartist demand for universal suffrage arose from political rather than economic causes.' How far do these extracts, and any other evidence known to you, support this assertion? (8 marks)

Summary Diagram
The Chartist Movement in 1839

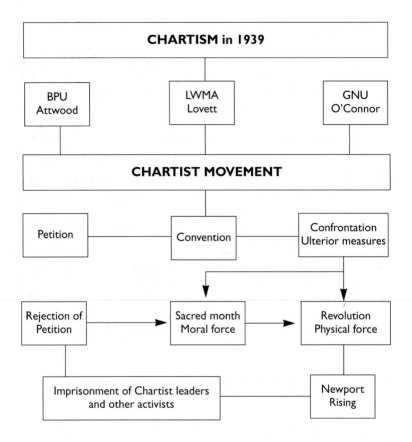

4 Chartism and the Chartists

For ten years, from 1838 to 1848, Chartism had been a significant aspect of the nation's political life. It had worried government as a threat to property, and as a cause of disaffection in many cities in the land, but never came close to persuading the political elite that the 1832 settlement should be re-examined or that political justice might require that the franchise should be widened. To many of the middle classes it was no more than a distant rumble of discontent, only perhaps made real in the 'defence' of London in 1848 (see pages 93-95). To the working classes, Chartism, with its evangelical flavour, promised a righting of ancient wrongs and the political means by which the majority, by securing the right to vote, would become full members of a society from which for so long they had been excluded. As equal members of that society, they also glimpsed the chance of correcting contemporary, as well as ancient wrongs.

This chapter will seek to answer some of the many questions which arise from any study of this complex movement. Who, for instance, were the Chartists, and why, at least at the national level, did Chartism appear as a single-sex movement? The Chartists always claimed that they were a national movement, and not a bundle of local discontents only held together by a common platform. Does an examination of Chartism bear this out? If its origins were so diverse and its support groups equally so, is it really possible to see a genuine unity underpinning the political programme to which they all subscribed?

1 Members and Supporters

a) England

In any political movement, a distinction has to be drawn between those who are sympathisers - and who will turn out on special occasions - and those who are committed workers for the cause. This was particularly true of Chartism, for known membership could lead to persecution, to dismissal from employment and to obstacles put in the way of any new employment. So those who were the activists were most likely to be 'independent' - artisans, shoe-makers, tailors, shopkeepers, publicans, lecturers, journalists.

Industrial England in the 1830s and 1840s was a network of small communities, each with its own distinct economic activity. Nottingham was surrounded by stocking- and lace-making districts. Leicester and the nearby villages had glove-making. Lancashire was dominated by cotton, as Yorkshire was by the woollen industry. Northampton was the centre of the shoe-making industry. In all these areas, capitalist production was taking hold, threatening long-standing practices and agreements, a threat often unsuccessfully challenged by strike action. To those at risk, whose only property was their labour or their skill, Chartism seemed to offer a means by which they could regain some control over their own conditions of employment.

The bulk of Chartist support came from England's major industry, textiles. Within that industry, the hand-loom weavers formed a large part of Chartism's supporters. They ranged from the carpet weavers in Kidderminster, worsted weavers in Bradford, and linen weavers in Barnsley to silk weavers in Spitalfields. As a class, whether out-workers at home or employees in a factory, they were gradually being replaced by power-looms and as a consequence suffering a reduction in pay and in status. As Dorothy Thompson argues, 'it was not in most cases under-employment or unemployment which caused their poverty, but the fact that a full day's work, sometimes by a whole family, did not produce a subsistence wage'.[1] What these Chartists wanted was protection by the State to ensure a living wage for their skilled trade.

Dorothy Thompson emphasises that 'weavers by hand or power-loom were the largest occupational group recorded among the Chartists',[2] and from their ranks also came local and national leaders, the speakers and the officers of the movement. Another widely-represented group were the Lancashire cotton spinners, who appear amongst the lists of Chartist prisoners and of subscribers to the Land Plan but rarely emerge as officers or leaders, no doubt because, like farm labourers, they were more easily identified and consequently victimised.

Throughout the entire Chartist period, tradesmen of all kinds were active in the movement. By far the largest group were the shoe-makers, ranging from the local cobbler to the highly skilled craftsman who made shoes for the luxury trade. Traditionally radical as a class, they were particularly strong in London where they ranked as one of the largest occupational groups committed to Chartism. A similarly strong presence can be found in towns as different in social structure as Brighton or Sheffield. Tailors were another significant minority who often appear in lists of Chartist committees or officers. Like hand-loom weavers, they looked to a successful Chartist movement to provide that protection for their trade which government had failed to supply. One London tailor, William Cuffey, the son of a West Indian slave, had taken part in the aborted rising in 1848 and had been sentenced to 21 years transportation (see page 105).

Many other tradesmen figure in the ranks of Chartism. Blacksmiths appear not only as using their skills to make pikes for Chartist demonstrations but also as local leaders. There are also silversmiths, watchmakers, metal-workers, and woodworkers such as carpenters and joiners. From the building trade came stone-masons and bricklayers. Like many other workers in early Victorian England, they too had cause for concern. In particular, their status and conditions were being eroded by the growth of speculative house building, mainly in brick rather than in stone. This led to an increase in the number of unskilled casual workers, who were bitterly resented and resisted by the traditional craftsmen in the building industry.

A common thread running through all these trades was the uncertainty that a fast changing society was bringing into their lives. The vagaries of the market was one very important element in this. Britain was now moving with increasing rapidity from a relatively stable and insulated economy to one open to the world market and subject to changes both unexpected and uncontrollable. One primary economic factor affecting the rise and fall of Chartism which can be readily identified is the immediate distress caused by a sudden slump in trade and the consequent cut-back in the work-force. But another - and this is long term rather than short term - is the disruption in settled practices within any industry caused by the removal of protection offered either by the state or by long-established custom. When the state failed to respond to petitioning or to pleas from those affected, many were to see their remedy as the seizure of the levers of power.

Protection of the artisan by the state had effectively been ended in 1814 with the repeal of the Elizabethan Statute of Artificers. This had given local JPs the power to fix wage rates and had also required that all those entering a given trade should have been through a period of apprenticeship sufficient to allow a master-craftsman time to pass on his skill to his apprentice. This legally enforced requirement was fundamental in a society where no other form of training existed. For the artisan it was analogous to the restriction on entry practised by middle-class professions such as the law. Hence, the abolition of state-controlled apprenticeship and the erosion of wage rates fixed by custom, rather than by the market, undermined the status of all skill-based employment. It permitted the entry of casual unskilled labour into hitherto secure and proudly maintained crafts, thereby forcing down wage rates. This fundamental change in status was to be an important recruiting factor in the Chartist movement.

The plight of the weavers in particular led the mill-owner MP John Fielden to propose to Parliament in 1834 that local trade boards should be empowered to fix a minimum wage, subject to periodic review. As a delaying tactic, a Parliamentary Select Committee was appointed to consider this proposal and, as a consequence of its favourable report, a bill was introduced first in 1835, and then again in 1836 and 1837. To block such a reform a Royal Commission was appointed steered by sound free market men which reported bleakly that 'the power of the Czar of Russia could not raise the wages of men so situate'.[3] Such a judgement summed up the dominant economic philosophy of the day that nothing must be done which hindered the operation of the market - in wages as well as in goods. The effect of all this, in E. P. Thompson's view, is that 'it transformed the weavers into confirmed physical force Chartists'.[4]

b) Scotland

Scottish Chartism exemplified on a smaller scale many of the main characteristics of the movement in the South. It developed rapidly in Scotland's industrial heartland, in Glasgow and the surrounding area, where her main industries, metal, mining and textiles were concentrated and where - as in England - a working man found that 'the cheaper it became to produce the necessities of life, the longer he seemed to have to labour for bare existence, and the benefits seemed to accumulate in the hands of a few'.[5] Again, universal suffrage had long been seen as the only means by which the people's grievances could be addressed. However, in one significant respect, the movement in Scotland differed from its English counterpart, in that religion and the churches had a continuous influence on its development.

Glasgow could reasonably claim to be the true birthplace of Chartism rather than Birmingham, for it was there that the famous meeting of 21 May 1838 held to campaign on behalf of the transported cotton spinners (see page 30) saw the launch of the National Petition for the 'People's Charter'. Between that date and the Birmingham meeting on 6 August, O'Connor toured Scotland, anxious to win over Scottish supporters to his own alliance, the Great Northern Union. By the early months of 1839, Scottish Chartism was in strong voice, with more than 130 local association and its first newspaper, the *True Scotsman*. When, in February, the Chartist Convention met in London, Scotland sent several delegates, including Dr John Taylor, a firm believer in direct action. His bellicose stance affronted many of the other Scottish delegates, some of whom as a consequence abandoned the meeting and returned home. It was he and the youthful Harney who emerged as the advocates of the necessity for physical force to secure the Charter. Taylor's readiness to move to the 'ultimate measure' was exceptional amongst Scottish Chartists, who had in a public debate voted unanimously against it

With the rejection of the 1839 petition, local leaders diversified the movement in several ways, seeking other means by which pressure could be brought to bear against opponents in state and society. 'Exclusive dealing' (see page 118) was common, sometimes leading to the founding of co-operative stores in Chartist areas. As in England, Temperance Chartism took hold, as a means of denying revenue to the Treasury, but with increased force in a population which at least nominally was traditionally more puritanical. In many towns, Chartist total abstinence societies flourished and well-known Chartists headed appeals to fellow working men to abandon drink.

In Scotland, 'exclusive dealing' took a unique form in that it was used against those Established Church and Baptist clergymen who showed themselves hostile to Chartism. By 1840, Chartists began to organise Sunday services and called themselves 'Christian Chartist

Churches'. The democratic basis of Chartism - so clearly shown in the organisation of the National Charter Association - was reflected in the practice of calling each member of the congregation in turn to be chairman of the church. As Alexander Wilson points out, 'the Chartist church movement was a manifestation of the deeply religious spirit which pervaded the Scottish Chartist agitation'.[6]

The National Charter Association's policy of submitting Chartist candidates in the general election of July 1841 was adopted in Scotland where seven candidates were victorious at the hustings (see page 73-4) but failed at the polls. In Glasgow, some of the electors who were also Chartists followed the O'Connorite line and voted for the Tory candidate - to the lasting disgust of the local radical press.

In 1842, the Complete Suffrage movement divided Scottish Chartists. When the Sturge conference opened in Birmingham on 27 December, there were 421 Scottish towns or villages represented, with those unable to meet a delegate's expenses represented by Scots living in Birmingham. Although the Conference failed, Complete Suffragism persisted in Scotland well into 1843 and helped to nurture those whom Harney dubbed 'traitors and deserters, still having the unblushing assurance to call themselves Chartists'.

After the divergences of 1842, Scottish Chartism never really recovered its former strength. However, there were Scottish delegates at the 1848 Convention who spoke movingly of the distress in Scotland while counselling moderation. Ernest Jones followed up the Kennington Common meeting by touring Scotland with proposals for a Memorial to the Queen - with hints that, if this failed, other measures would have to be taken. But Scottish Chartism was in serious decline, quickened by the authorities' action in charging four Chartists with sedition. The trials themselves were in stark contrast to those held in England, and were carried out with exemplary fairness. Of the four, one was acquitted and the other three were sentenced to three months imprisonment.

As in England, individual Chartists reappeared as activists in the new reform associations which marked the 1860s. The Scottish National Reform League, founded in 1866, had ex-Chartists such as James Moir and Robert Cochran as prominent members. One of their largest meetings, with an audience estimated as well over a 100,000, was held on Glasgow Green, with Moir and Cochran in the platform party, together with Ernest Jones and John Bright, all united in a call for manhood suffrage and the secret ballot.

c) Wales

In Wales, as in England, one of the significant factors in the growth of Chartism was the agitation against the New Poor Law. Yet another was the influence of Welsh Nonconformity in a society where, by 1851, three-quarters of the population were Nonconformist. Three areas in particular emerge as strong Chartist centres: Carmarthen and neighbouring Llanelly, Merthyr Tydfil and the Welsh textile towns of Welshpool and Newtown.

In Carmarthen, the leader was a local solicitor, Hugh Williams, related by marriage to the Anti-Corn Law Leaguer Richard Cobden and a partner with Cobden in several business enterprises. Williams was to be one of the three Welsh delegates to the 1839 People's Convention. In Merthyr, David John, blacksmith and a Unitarian pastor, and his two sons were prominent in the Chartist movement and founder members of the Merthyr Working Men's Association (WMA) when it was established in 1839. In mid-Wales, Thomas Powell, another middle-class man, was the local leader when a WMA was founded there.

In Monmouthshire, the fast growing town of Newport set up a WMA in 1839 and a prosperous local draper, John Frost, was elected as an area delegate to the Convention. In the adjacent coal fields, Chartism took rapid root and new Associations sprang up, many fuelled by grievances peculiar to the social and economic structure of the mining industry (whose problems are examined in detail in Chapter 4).

Wales, in the Chartist period, was a predominantly rural society, with pockets of traditional industry such as the manufacture of woollen garments together with the new ironworks and coal mines worked by men noted for their independence of spirit. Wales provided ready listeners and converts to the promises of the Charter. It also was the scene of what has been called the 'Last Rising', that in Newport, which some historians have argued was intended to be no more than a 'monster demonstration' (see pages 45-8).

After the grim fiasco of Newport, Chartism never again regained its former strength in Wales. However, with the formation of the National Charter Association in 1840, a Merthyr Tydfil man, Morgan Williams, was elected to its executive and was a delegate to the Convention in 1841. He stood at the Merthyr hustings as a Chartist candidate in the General Election in 1841 and used this opportunity to explain the Chartist case.

It was Morgan Williams again who represented the Merthyr area in the April 1842 Convention. The Complete Suffrage Union, centred in Birmingham, with its programme of limited reform, reached out to Merthyr district where a large meeting passed a resolution in its favour. However, the summer months of 1842 were marked by a downturn in the local economy, with strikes at Cyfarthia and Dowlais ironworks and iron-masters dismissing known Chartists. There were reports of workmen's clubs buying arms and talk of more extreme measures, but there was no fresh revolt. Instead there were meetings to campaign on behalf of Frost, the Newport Chartist transported to Australia for his part in the Newport Rising.

The failure of the London Convention in April 1848 led to a protest meeting in Merthyr's market square, but no action was proposed - or for that matter seemed feasible. Chartism in Wales disappeared in

1848; effectively it never recovered from the disaster of 1839. In the years following, it had neither the unity nor the strength of purpose which marked the earlier years.

Welsh Chartism had evolved either as a result of London-based lecturers arousing the country or, as in mid-Wales, as a direct result of the intervention of the Birmingham Political Union and its travelling lecturers. After 1839, with its local leaders in prison or in Australian convict settlements, it rapidly dissolved into a fragmentary protest movement, responding weakly to the prevailing economic winds of the day.

d) Ireland

The great contribution Ireland made to Chartism may be found from the movement's leaders, with O'Connor and O'Brien at its head, to the many Irishmen in its ranks, such as James Duffy, the Leeds Chartist. In Ireland itself, there was no significant Chartist association, although in Dublin, the Irish Universal Suffrage Association (IUSA), founded in 1841, collected signatures and sold the movement's newspaper. Branches were established in Belfast and other towns such as Newry. The IUSA committed itself to the Six Points as a sign of their support for English Chartism in their campaign to secure the Repeal of the Act of Union, the Act which in 1801 had abolished the Irish Parliament and established the United Kingdom of Great Britain and Ireland.

Chartists readily responded to the Irish cause and increasingly they linked the Charter to a call for Repeal. Irish history also played its part in forming Chartist political consciousness. There are records of Chartist groups touring the English manufacturing districts with a theatrical version of the trial of Robert Emmet, the Irishman executed for his part in the 1798 Rising. R.G. Gammage, the Chartist historian, claimed that one of the key events in his political education was reading Emmet's famous speech from the dock. For physical force Chartists, the 1798 Rising remained both an inspiration and a warning of what could happen if a rebellion in England should fail.

The two most prominent Irishmen of the day, Daniel O'Connell and Feargus O'Connor, fell out over O'Connell's hostility to trade unions and his support for the Poor Law Amendment Act. In Manchester, Irish labourers were recruited by the Anti-Corn Law League to break up Chartist meetings. But neither of these two events should be interpreted as evidence of a general Irish opposition to the Chartist movement amongst the Irish population in England. The great Irish cause was Repeal of the Union and to this end both O'Connellites and O'Connorites were committed. Where they differed was in the means by which this could be achieved. To Irish Chartists, the road to liberation lay through the suffrage: through Chartism, Ireland would achieve its freedom from the English yoke.

2 Women and Chartism

Chartist women, although so often acting in strong support to their menfolk, rarely emerged on the local platform and never appeared as national figures in the movement. At the time of the founding of the London Working Men's Association (LWMA), there had been talk of including women's suffrage in their manifesto but this was abandoned as likely to harm the call for universal male suffrage. What the LWMA feared was the widespread prejudice against women entering what was seen as a man's world. The LWMA itself had no women members.

That women were actively involved in the movement at grass-roots level is perhaps evidenced by the pamphlets which appeared urging the case for female suffrage. Two Chartists, R.J. Richardson and John Watkins, both wrote pamphlets arguing for a female franchise and for women's participation in political activity. Both, however, proposed a limitation on that right which would make it significantly less than universal: they excluded married women on the grounds that their interests coincided with their husbands and therefore no independent recognition was needed. William Lovett and his supporters in the 'New Move' (see page 75) included women's suffrage in their programme and increasingly by the 1840s, Chartists in general had come to assume that when the Charter became law, votes for women would soon follow.

Women were prominent in the great mass meetings held on the Yorkshire and Lancashire moors, in the processions which marked the earlier stages of the movement, and could also be heard egging on their men in protest crowds such as those in Nottingham in 1839, where the local paper, the *Nottingham Mercury*, described their behaviour as 'most flagrant and wicked in the extreme'. Of necessity, they were also responsible for carrying out the policy of 'exclusive dealing' as women controlled the family household budget. The *Northern Star* in August 1839 gives one example of women's attempts to spread the message in reporting on a Bradford women's organisation. It described their activities in these terms:

1   The female radicals of the Bradford district amounting to upward of 600, walked in procession through the principal streets headed by a band of music and banners ... at the head of the procession there was carried by a woman a large printed board with the words 'exclusive
5   dealing'.[7]

The general absence of working-class women from Chartist politics after 1840, as the new formal structure emerged, should not be interpreted as a lack of interest, for their loyalty was unquestionable. One significant factor is that meetings often took place in pubs, places where it was not customary for women to enter. Many other possible reasons suggest themselves, of which perhaps the most significant was a wife's natural hostility to meetings held where a husband's wages could so easily be frittered away! Another most certainly would be the difficulty of finding ways of safeguarding the children in a mother's absence.

In the early years of the movement, women's radical associations sprang up in many parts of the country, in all more than 100. Some towns such as Nottingham, Bradford and Newcastle had particularly active groups. To these Female Political Unions fell many of the supportive activities such as raising funds for the families of Chartists held in prison. They also ran Sunday schools and Chartist schools committed to bringing up children free of the culture of deference to their 'betters' which permeated the church schools. Again, they christened their children with the names of famous Chartists. However despite the evidence of such general commitment to the common cause, women did not participate in political activity as equals to men. Whereas in the women's organisations all office holders were women, in the mixed societies only one example has been traced of a woman holding office. And in the 1848 Petition, only eight per cent of the signatures were those of women. This disproportion reflects the subordinate role assigned to women in all classes of society. Any crossing over into traditional male territory had to wait until the general emancipation which the twentieth century was to bring.

3 The Nature of Chartism

Both contemporaries and historians have raised fundamental questions about the causes of the movement and about its nature. J.R. Stephens, the anti-Poor-Law campaigner, had proclaimed that 'Universal Suffrage was a knife and fork question'. To another contemporary, the great social critic Thomas Carlyle, Chartism formed part of what he termed 'the Condition of England question'. Writing in 1842, he affirmed that:

> Chartism means the bitter discontent grown fierce and mad, the wrong condition therefore or the wrong disposition, of the Working Classes of England.[8]

Mark Hovell, the first modern historian of Chartism, takes a not dissimilar view:

> social chartism was a protest against what existed, not a reasoned policy to set up anything in its place. Chartism was largely a passionate negation.[9]

More recently, G.D.H. Cole has argued that:

> the Chartist movement was essentially an economic movement with a purely political programme.[10]

All these assessments have a certain validity. In its beginnings,

Chartism arose from protests against seen injustices and from campaigns for social improvements. Professor Rostow's social tension chart (see page 9) sets out a clear link between periods of extreme distress and the peaks of the movement. Feargus O'Connor himself recognised that the movement more readily flourished during an economic downturn. And one of the many factors which help to account for the rapid decline of Chartism in the 1850s was the overall improvement in the British economy.

And yet all these generalisations do not catch Chartism's multi-faceted nature. For instance, the evidence of the nature and extent of Chartist culture undermines the assertion that it was merely 'a passionate negation'. Again, it clearly had more than a political programme as shown in Temperance or Christian Chartism or in its continuing concern for education.

a) Was Chartism a National Movement?

Essentially Chartism was an urban movement - or more specifically a movement which drew in a wide band of workers except workers on the land. To take an active part in protest politics was simply not feasible in the rural England of the mid-nineteenth century. Not only was there the simple difficulty of distance from the nearest town but, more oppressively, the certainty that any open statement of political intent would be under the hostile eye of farmer or squire and was likely to bring immediate retribution in the loss of job or tied cottage. In the recent past, the shires had erupted in open discontent, first with food riots, such as those in Littleport in 1817. Furthermore, the introduction of the threshing machine - a threat to winter work - had sparked off the Swing Riots of 1830-1, widespread in the southern and eastern counties. Again the common practice of poaching, despite the extremely harsh Game Laws (which imposed punishments as draconian as imprisonment or even transportation), indicates the rumbling discontent, arising from empty bellies, which lay beneath the feudal class relations of rural England. However, the bitter distress of the rural labourer was to play no part in Chartism. Rural discontent triggered off attacks on threshing machines or food riots, essentially primitive protest movements, but the field labourer was hampered by his own position within the social hierarchy from reaching the level of political organisation which his contemporary in the town could achieve. Under the paternalistic rule of parson and landowner, the rural worker, when the strain proved too much, resorted to the eighteenth-century remedy of riot and disorder.

The thesis that Chartism was no more than a protest movement based on the new working class of the northern textile towns conflicts with the evidence of extensive support from traditional artisans such as cobblers, tailors, and cabinet makers, who were amongst its most active supporters. And again, although it often appears to be a loose federation of regions, its essential regionalism was more a function of restrictive legislation than a reflection of the nature of the movement itself. In the aftermath of the French Revolution, successive British governments had passed laws which were intended to prevent the rise of a national political movement which might threaten the established order. What is true is that certain towns are more prominent in the history of Chartism than others: London, Glasgow, Birmingham, Leeds, and then in the 1840s London again, when both the *Northern Star* and the NCA made their headquarters in the capital. There was, of course, also the simple fact that London was the centre of government and the home of Parliament, which meant that as each petitioning movement peaked, London would be the focus of Chartist energies and activities.

What is remarkable is that, despite statutes aimed at curbing 'subversive' political movements, Chartism for almost a decade seemed to its followers - and certainly to the government - to be a national movement bringing together all working-class ambitions, thereby producing a temporary union of the excluded which could be interpreted as a threat to the established order. The Seditious Meetings Act of 1817 had prohibited permanent links between different branches, so that the NCA was never able to set up a democratic federal structure with a hierarchy of elected different regional councils. In essence, Chartism remained an association of local societies reflecting local interests, bound together by its lecturer-missionaries, the *Northern Star*, the Council, the Convention and above all by a common acceptance of the Charter.

As a national movement, Chartism had many similarities with early Methodism. Its smallest unit was a class of ten, with a leader charged with collecting subscriptions and with making a report to a monthly meeting. Based on this 'cell' were a number of Councils from local to county level, with a General Executive Committee as the supreme body. To meet the law's requirements, all local officers and district councillors were nominated rather than elected and then appointed by the National Executive. The only legally permitted use of the elective principle was when all members took part in an annual election to the Executive. Expenses for delegates to such bodies as the Convention were provided by collections at Chartist meetings or by subscriptions from trade societies to a common fund known as the 'National Rent'.

Chartism developed one other institution: the Convention. The Birmingham Political Union had first hit upon this strategy as in law a Convention was deemed legal provided it was a petitioning body. A further stipulation was that delegates could be elected (rather than nominated) if the election took place in public at the hustings. The first Convention, which met in 1839, was from its inception seen as the 'People's Parliament' and as a true democratic alternative to the existing House of Commons. In the new formal structure reflected in the establishment of the NCA in 1840, provision was made for an annual Convention. However, not until 1843 was this generally accepted, as some Chartists felt that such an overseeing body weakened rather than strengthened the movement.

What ran through Chartism was a continuing insistence on a democratic structure which nevertheless must remain within the narrow confines of the law. The practice of the Anti-Corn Law League provides an interesting contrast. Its governing body was a non-elected council, with membership available to anyone who had donated £50 or more (a very considerable sum in mid-Victorian terms) to the League. No attempt was made to offer even a pretence of democratic control.

b) Was Chartism Essentially a Political Movement?

E.P. Thompson sums up the Chartist movement in these words:

> The line from 1832 to Chartism is not a haphazard pendulum alternation of 'political' and 'economic' agitation, but a direct progression, in which simultaneous and related movements converge towards a single point. This point was the vote.[11]

This 'point' had been the objective of the earlier working-class radical movements such as the Hampden Clubs (see page 10) and the post-1815 campaigns for universal suffrage, and Chartism inherited both their techniques and their fundamental aims. Some of those who were to emerge as Chartist front-runners had cut their teeth in the 1832 Reform Bill agitation and saw themselves as continuing a fight which had only partly been won. The 'betrayal' of 1832 and the harshly oppressive legislation such as the New Poor Law which followed (see pages 19-20) only confirmed their conviction that the franchise offered the *only* salvation. There were many grievances, national as well as local, that the movement gathered up in its progress but, with the exception of Corn Law Repeal and the repeal of the Irish Act of Union, the Charter remained the sole and constant objective.

This 'point' reflected also various concerns which surfaced at different times in the Chartists' campaign. Perhaps most important was their claim that justice required that they should be given the right to vote, for without this badge of citizenship they were excluded from full participation in the political nation. This call for political equality remained a permanent theme in Chartist rhetoric, echoing the late eighteenth-century insistence on the Rights of Man and on Natural Rights.

Underpinning these political demands was the certainty that the social changes which the working class saw as essential - such as a limitation on factory hours - could only be achieved through political power. From the standpoint of the enfranchised property-owning class, Macaulay, the great Whig historian, was equally clear that any political concessions to the Chartist would be a threat to property. If we interpret 'property' as including both wealth and profits, then this fear was well-founded. For instance, any change in the pattern of the working day might well limit the profitability of a textile mill by failing to make full use of costly plant.

Chartists such as Bronterre O'Brien saw the problem quite differently. He asserted:

> it is because you are unrepresented that you have no property...your poverty is the result not the cause of your being unrepresented.[12]

With O'Brien a new and positive socialist note began to appear. O'Connor was, as he said himself, never a socialist. After the withdrawal of O'Connor, Chartism aligned itself with continental socialism and a redistributive political philosophy which proposed that wealth should be more fairly divided within society. If, before 1848, Chartism had been an implicit threat to 'property', after 1848 the threat was made explicit.

References

1   Dorothy Thompson, *The Chartists* (Temple Smith, 1984), p. 112.
2   Ibid, p. 209.
3   E.P. Thompson, *The Making of the English Working Class* (Penguin, 1974), p. 333.
4   Ibid, p. 333.
5   Alexander Wilson, *The Chartist Movement in Scotland* (Manchester University Press,1970), p. 18.
6   Ibid, p. 150.
7   Dorothy Thompson, *The Chartists*, p. 135.
8   Gareth Steadman Jones, 'The Language of Chartism' in *The Chartist Experience: Studies in Working-Class Radicalism and Culture 1830-60* edited by James Epstein and Dorothy Thompson (Macmillan, 1952), p. 3.
9   Ibid, p. 10.
10 Ibid, p. 10.
11 Ibid, p. 11.
12 A. Plummer, *Bronterre* (George Allen and Unwin, 1971) pp. 177-8.

Answering essay questions on 'Chartism and the Chartists'

1. Do you agree that Chartism was 'essentially an economic movement'?

This question on the nature of Chartism is asking you to weigh up the evidence for and against this judgement. In some form or another, this is a favourite question and one on which you need to have a clearly worked out essay plan before beginning to tackle it.

Do you agree with Carlyle and with historians such as Mark Hovell? Rostow's social tension chart seems to support Carlyle by suggesting a clear link between times of economic depression and Chartist activity. Is this, however, sufficient reason to accept his verdict? After all, didn't the Chartist leaders themselves recognise that the bad times spurred on the movement to heightened activity? But doesn't Bronterre O'Brien by linking poverty with political exclusion make a similar point to Carlyle: that the movement is powered by economic injustice and that the means to solve the problem was at hand? Isn't it also quite clear that many Chartists saw the vote as the only way to improve the conditions under which they lived and worked? On the other hand, there is the possibility that a downturn in the economy served only to fan the embers, rather than light the fire. Here you might wish to examine the evidence based upon the long established political tradition which saw the vote as the badge of equal citizenship. Might it be relevant here to consider the essentially political origins of the Charter itself? And again, is there the evidence of a flourishing Chartist counter-culture reflected in their involvement in activities ranging from lectures and discussion groups to carnivals and processions?

Source-based questions on 'Chartism and the Chartists'

1. The Nature of Chartism
Read the three extracts on page 63.
- **a)** Define briefly the following references:
  - i) 'wrong disposition' (line 32 on page 63), (2 marks)
  - ii) 'passionate negation' (lines 37-38 on page 63). (2 marks)
- **b)** How far does the view expressed in the third extract reflect a widely-held Chartist conviction? (6 marks)
- **c)** Is the second extract fundamentally in agreement with the first? (7 marks)
- **d)** 'Chartism aimed to turn the world upside down'. To what extent do these extracts, and any other evidence known to you, support this assertion? (8 marks)

5 The National Charter Association and its Rivals

With its leaders in prison, together with many hundreds of the rank and file, by the beginning of 1840 Chartism looked as if it had run its course. Yet within a short time, the movement had re-formed once more and was mounting a national petition to Parliament. This chapter begins by examining that process. It goes on to consider Chartism's relationship with the Anti-Corn League, its electoral strategy and the proposed cross-class alliance with Joseph Sturge and the Complete Suffrage Union. It ends with an assessment of the failure of the 1842 Petition and the 1842 strikes in mining and manufacturing .

1 The Imprisoned Leader

O'Connor remained a prisoner in York until August 1841. To begin with, he was held in conditions similar to any other convict, except that he had the privilege of wearing his own clothes. Throughout the country, mass meetings were organised on his behalf seeking a removal of some of the restrictions imposed upon him. Within a short time, the Whig Home Secretary, Lord Normanby, modified O'Connor's regime and allowed him his own food and wine. Although he was forbidden to write political articles, nevertheless O'Connor successfully evaded this restriction and continued to write for the *Northern Star*.

While in prison, O'Connor's standing in the movement grew. He was widely seen as the leader who had been victimised, his only 'crime' that of publishing Chartists' speeches in the *Northern Star*. In the Chartist press, he outlined his ideas on how the movement could be strengthened and reformed. The time seemed ripe for a fresh initiative. As early as August 1839, Scottish delegates, meeting in Glasgow, had set up a Central Committee for Scotland and appointed paid lecturers to tour the country. Similar moves were made in Newcastle, in London and in South Lancashire. George Julian Harney had been recruited as one of the band of Scottish lecturers and he floated the idea that an organisation similar to that in Scotland should be established for England. His key proposal was that there should be a full-time national executive.

The outcome of this series of local initiatives was the conference of 23 delegates which met in Manchester on 20 July 1840 and founded the National Charter Association (NCA). O'Connor had enthusiastically supported the calling of the conference and had outlined a plan by which funding could be found to pay lecturers and to provide the expenses for delegate conferences and for a permanent executive.

2 The National Charter Association

Whereas in 1839 Chartist organisation had reached its peak with the Convention - essentially a temporary organisation with shifting membership - from the outset the NCA had an Executive Council with seven full-time salaried members, including a secretary and a treasurer. Executive Council members, who were elected annually, were also to act as Chartist missionaries. There was an elaborate democratic structure covering all parts of the country and membership was open to all who paid a small membership fee. Within the context of the time, as James Epstein points out, this new form of organisation reflects ' a general trend towards more sophisticated forms of working-class association, characterised by regular subscriptions and the election and regular payment of permanemt officials'.[1] Similar moves were taking place in the Friendly Societies or within trade unions such as the Miners' Association, founded in 1842.

One grave limitation on the new organisation was the 1817 Seditious Meetings Act, introduced to prevent the formation of nation-wide revolutionary movements. This act prohibited the establishment of individual branches of any national association - with the assumption that local branches might consist of activists - and imposed the requirement that all members' names should be registered. As a consequence, the original plan was amended, local branches as such disappeared, and all members were deemed to belong solely to a single national body.

Despite these impediments, however, many local groups were brought within the NCA, and by April 1842 there were around 50,000 members scattered in 401 localities. As the National Petition in 1842 had more than three million signatures, it is clear that the NCA represented no more than an active nucleus of the Chartist movement. Fear of government reprisals and, in depressed areas, the cost of membership fees would hold back some potential supporters. And again all parties have their hard-core supporters and a less active mass of well-wishers. In this respect, as in so many others, the NCA must be seen as the forerunner of a modern party, but, more than any modern counterpart, it was hampered by law and by a society in which the politics of deference - the sense that some were natural rulers - still played an important part.

3 The Chartists and the Anti-Corn Law League

In its second phase, Chartism was to face a major rival for popular support in the Anti-Corn Law League (ACL). Founded in 1838 and based in Manchester, it was headed by two famous radical MPs, Richard Cobden and John Bright. By 1841, the League had a national organisation, a band of paid travelling lecturers, and the backing of much of the manufacturing interest. Essentially it was a middle-class pressure group, with a limited aim: the repeal of the Corn Laws - the abolition of protection on a single commodity. In this sense it had only one natural enemy: the agricultural interest - the landowners and farmers who were seen as the sole beneficiaries of a system which protected British agriculture from foreign competition by duties on imported corn. On the other hand, the Chartists, a working-class organisation, might be seen as confronting the whole of established society, the propertied and enfranchised classes. The League differed also from its rival in one other important respect in that, in general, it was not short of funds to pursue any strategy which would achieve its purpose.

While Chartism was intent on constitutional reform and the League had a simple economic aim, nevertheless past demands for the vote had often been linked with repeal of the Corn Laws, which were widely seen as responsible for high food prices. At Peterloo, and again during the Reform Bill crisis, both reforms had been called for. Would a common interest perhaps bridge the gap between the Chartists and the League?

One major obstacle was the social gulf between classes in mid-Victorian society. Middle-class observers such as the correspondent from Clayton, near Bradford, cited by Dorothy Thompson, often saw only depravity in the lower classes.

1   In the township there are 14 beer shops - in these strongholds of the
     devil, shunned and detested by every honest man, every description of
     knavery is carried on and villainy concocted...card playing and gambling
     are carried on from morning to night without any attempt at secrecy ...
5   I have heard it said that since the establishment of beer shops wicked-
     ness has been alarmingly augmented, a consequence of the practices at
     those places.[2]

Mark Hovell, whose pioneering work on Chartism was published in 1918, was the first professional historian to work on the Chartist movement, and he echoes a similar tone. In writing of the anti-Poor Law movement, he describes its supporters in this way:

1   The rank and file were men already desperate by continuous and
     increasing poverty, ignorant and unlettered men deprived or fearing to
     be deprived, of a resource on which they had long counted, men coars-
     ened by evil surroundings and brutalised by hard and unremitting toil,
5   relieved only by periods of unemployment in which their dulled minds
     brooded over their misfortunes and recalled their lost prosperity.[3]

Both these assessments use highly emotive language to depict what the writers see as the nature of working-class life. In the first, 'knavery' and 'villainy' stigmatise leisure pursuits such as gambling and card playing which were almost universal in upper-class England. Again, middle-class fears would be aroused by vague reference to an increase in unspecified 'wickedness'. In Mark Hovell, terms such as 'ignorant and unlettered men', 'coarsened', 'brutalised', with 'their dulled minds', are used to conjure up a general vision of working-class life which has little to do with the reality of the Chartist movement, the trade societies or the small savers in the Friendly Societies.

On their side, working-class Chartists were suspicious of middle-class motives. Although at first, some Chartists had supported repeal of the Corn Laws, they became increasingly concerned that repeal and a possible fall in the price of bread would be seized on by employers as a reason for reducing wages. Consequently anti-Bread Tax Chartists began to argue that repeal must be linked with factory legislation controlling hours and wages.

The case against Corn Law Repeal was made out by O'Connor himself. England's need, as he saw it, was to achieve self-sufficiency in agriculture. Not only should the farmer be protected but there should be a move away from the towns and back to the land. Resettling town workers on small farms was essential for the future of society as a means of increasing agricultural production and as a way of providing a more fulfilling life for alienated industrial workers. Such convictions were later to lead him to launch the Chartist Land Plan (see pages 87-90).

If perhaps the fundamental difference between the League and the Chartists lay in what each saw as the necessary first step towards social improvment, class perceptions also played a part. Lucy Brown makes the point that the antagonism between the two organisations owed much to the *Northern Star* and the 'aggressive proletarianism of its tone' which 'fostered a general contempt for the middle classes'.[4] The other side of this coin, as she suggests, was an insistence that 'membership of the working class' was a 'matter for pride rather than self-pity'.[5]

If the social origins and the goals of the two movements were widely disparate, at times the language and tactics used often seemed remarkably similar. At Barnsley, a lecturer from the League was reported as summing up the aristocracy in these terms:

1 He described them as gluttonous and debauchees, as men who would not profit by the advantages with which they were surrounded, who impoverished the poor tenants to fill their capacious maws [greedy stomachs], and whose whole life is a routine of oppression, extravagance
5 and luxury, which terminates in the grave ...[6]

Compare this with Bronterre O'Brien in full flight:

1 Every lawyer in the country can vote - every thief of them - but did any one of this gang add a stiver [small coin] to the wealth of the nation? ... cotton-lords who possess all the skill and trickery and daring and effrontery of the pick-pocket, the burglar, and the highwayman rolled into one
5 - they all have votes, but not the working people.[7]

Again, Chartism often tried to disrupt meetings of the League. A local free trade newspaper in Huddersfield described what happened in one such meeting:

1 The conduct of the universal suffragemen, during the discussion, was such as to excite the unmitigated disgust of every well-regulated mind...Everything in the shape of argument or appeal to the facts was denounced as lies - the most ribald abuse of the speakers was indulged
5 in, and they were clamoured down by hooting, hissing, stamping on the floor, and every other species of unmanly annoyance.[8]

To deal with this tactic, Cobden recruited Manchester working-class free-traders into a new body, the Operative Anti-Corn Law Association, stiffened on occasion by Irish labourers, described by the historian Norman McCord as 'tough and rough'; people who would expect payment for their night's work. These 'defensive' measures resulted in such scenes as these in a meeting in October 1841 in Manchester, when a Chartist moved an amendment to the main resolution:

1 One speech in support was listened to, the second was refused a hearing. Mr Acland then spoke in support of the original motion, but was interrupted by a Chartist in the centre of the room. Upon this, a body of Irish rose. A cry of 'Put him out' was raised, and presently a forest of
5 shillelaghs [stout sticks] was seen flourishing in the air. The forms were upset, and the sides of several were torn off, and converted into short-staves. In attempting to gain the door several parties were overturned, and lay struggling in heaps on the floor.[9]

In the widespread strikes in the summer of 1842, the League also played a part by using agitators to try to goad hungry workers to the brink of revolution in order to force the government to yield to their demands for Repeal (see pages 78-90).

4 The 1841 General Election

In May 1841, defeated on a vote of confidence, the Melbourne government called a general election for the summer. For the Chartists, this was the first opportunity to put to the test Bronterre O'Brien's electoral plan - and to try to increase the number of Radical MPs who were Chartist sympathisers. O'Brien, like O'Connor, an Irish barrister, had first outlined his scheme to the 1839 Convention and delegates had accepted it as one of a package of 'ulterior measures'. They resolved that:

1 they will provide themselves with *chartist candidates*, so as to be prepared to propose them for their representatives at the next general election; and, if returned by a *show of hands*, such candidates to consider themselves veritable representatives of the people - to meet in London
5 at a time hereafter to be determined on.[10]

This proposal hinged on the archaic electoral practice of mid-nineteenth century England in which a platform called the 'hustings' was raised on nomination day and from which each candidate addressed the crowd who customarily turned up to listen to them. In a contested election, the returning officer would call for a show of hands (and many in the crowd who had no vote would raise their hands) and could then decide the result on this basis alone. If, however, a defeated candidate called for a poll, the law required that this must be held and then only registered electors could vote.

O'Brien himself took advantage of this unreformed system when, although held prisoner in Lancaster Castle, he stood for election in Newcastle and published an election address commended by Mark Hovell as a 'good and sensible document' which 'might have been written by Cobbett'.[11] He described himself as a 'Conservative Radical Reformer standing for peace, liberty, justice and order for all, founded on the freely expressed will of the majority' and calling for the radical reform of 'all that is unsound in our institutions'.[12] The result was a curious reflection of the electoral system of the day. O'Brien was elected by a show of hands and, as no poll was taken, he claimed he was one of the chosen representatives. Nevertheless the other two candidates, a Whig and a Tory, were declared elected. The legal costs required to challenge this result proved too high for local Chartists, so the two improperly elected MPs were returned. Seven other Chartists stood as 'hustings' candidates in widely differing constituencies such as Carlisle, Tynemouth and Marylebone. At Northampton, the Chartist Peter McDouall claimed election by a show of hands but came bottom of the poll.

O'Connor was careful not to dissociate himself from O'Brien's plan but he recognised that, as it was unlikely that this would be widely adopted, the movement must devise alternative strategies. For the small minority of Chartists who had the vote, the Nottingham by-election in April 1841 was evidence of what could be achieved. There local Chartists had marched en masse to the polls, voted for the Tory, John Walter, the proprietor of *The Times*, as the anti-Poor Law candi-date and helped to end the 35 years of Whig control of the constituency. To Chartist leaders, and in particular O'Connor, what now seemed possible was to bring down the hated Whigs. He called on Chartist voters 'in every instance where you have the power, return Tories instead of Whigs'. For O'Connor this was merely a question of tactical voting, summed up in his call 'to vote boldly against the devils, by voting for the devils in hell'.[13] At the same time O'Connor was not blind to the realities of the situation and he was anxious to see in Parliament a nucleus of MPs sympathetic to Chartism. Consequently where such men were standing, he called on Chartist voters to support them: candidates such as Sharman Crawford at Rochdale and John Arthur Roebuck at Bath - in some sense an early example of a cross-class alliance.

For many Chartists, O'Connor's advice to vote Tory was anathema and a betrayal of his former abstentionist stance. Bronterre O'Brien in particular, who ranked with O'Connor as a national leader, found this policy reversal unacceptable. The *Northern Star* published the sharp exchanges between the two. Neither gave any ground and these differences, increasingly personal, led finally to a breakdown in their relationship.

5 William Lovett and the 'New Move'

Lovett's year in Warwick Gaol was spent in radically different circumstances from O'Connor's imprisonment and at first the Home Secretary, Lord John Russell, would allow Lovett no privileges at all. Lobbying by radical MPs produced a slight improvement in diet and, perhaps more importantly, he was allowed writing materials.

While in Warwick, he wrote *Chartism* in which he reiterated his conviction that the People's Charter was essential for the creation of a just society. However, what was new was his emphasis on an educational programme, to be funded by a penny a week subscription from all Chartists who had signed the National Petition. The scheme was comprehensive, running from primary schools to high schools, with schools becoming adult education centres in the evening. And finally, Lovett proposed that a National Association should be founded to put these ideas into practice.

In March 1841, Lovett made his 'New Move' when he and 73 supporters published his plan for a National Association (NA). There were many of his old Chartist friends amongst the signatories, including Henry Hetherington and Henry Vincent. O'Connor and his immediate circle derided Lovett's proposals, labelling the group 'Knowledge Chartists'. As Joel Wiener points out, 'what was implied by the launching of the NA - and O'Connor understood this - was the possibility of an alliance between the new organisation and the middle classes'.[14]

Although the National Association seemed a significant threat to Chartist unity, it never really got off the ground. It lasted only to 1849, never rose above 500 members, and its grand plan for national education produced only a Sunday school and a single National Association Hall in Holborn. However, Lovett and the NA were to figure prominently, albeit briefly, in the most important attempt to create a cross-class alliance, the Complete Suffrage Union set up by Joseph Sturge.

6 The Complete Suffrage Union

Joseph Sturge, the founder of the Complete Suffrage Union (CSU), was a Birmingham Quaker, a corn importer, and an influential member of what came to be called the 'Moral Radical Party'. He had been a member of the BPU and he had been in the forefront of the campaign to emancipate the slaves in the West Indian colonies. He emerged as the spokesman of the rising Nonconformists industrial and commercial class and as the most persistent advocate of fundamental change in Church and State.

In October 1841, the *Nonconformist* newspaper, effectively the voice of the anti-establishment party, published a series of articles called 'Reconciliation betweeen the Middle and Working Classes' in which the term 'complete suffrage' was first used. Joseph Sturge took up the idea and at several Anti-Corn Law meetings in that winter he linked Repeal with 'complete suffrage'. At a League conference in Manchester in November, he secured a sympathetic hearing for his view at a specially-held post-Conference meeting. Richard Cobden, however, was hostile to any connection with Chartism even in a diluted form, but John Bright was more favourable. Cobden, like O'Connor when faced with Lovett's break-away group, was anxious lest a third force emerge in politics which would reduce support for the Anti-Corn Law League.

One important strand in early Victorian society which played a part in the creation of the CSU was the urge for self-improvement. One obvious aspect of this was education and the Chartist leader, William Lovett, had already published his own plans for working-class education, and had set up the National Association (see page 75). Temperance was another. Drink was widely seen as the scourge of the working class, and Chartists such as Henry Vincent in his Teetotal Chartist Association united a campaign for abstinence with the Charter, thus seeking both self-improvement and political change. Evangelical Christianity was a third, and in Birmingham, for instance, John Collins (who had been in prison with Lovett) had opened the Newhall Street Christian Chartist Church. Although these groups represented diversions from the main Chartist programme, none abandoned the Six Points; self-improvement was essentially an embellishment, not a distraction.

Although, when in March 1842 Sturge chaired a preliminary meeting in Birmingham, there were only three Nonconformist ministers in the platform party, he had also secured the backing of another 100 pastors, all of whom had signed the complete suffrage declaration. He appealed for support 'from all classes and regions'. On 5 April, the CSU held its first conference. The working-class members who had responded were all Chartists disillusioned with O'Connor: William Lovett, John Collins, Henry Vincent and Bronterre O'Brien. John Bright came with other Leaguers, together with famous 'Moral Radicals' such as Edward Miall, owner-editor of the *Nonconformist*. The meeting resolved to form the Complete Suffrage Union (which Sturge was to manage) and, in addition, the Chartists present were successful in having all Six Points of the Charter accepted as policy. Adopting the familiar Chartist pattern, the CSU sent out 'missionaries' to set up sister associations. By the end of 1842, there were 90 in all, with a bunching in Scotland, where all the small towns had sizeable branches. In Paisley, for instance, there were 5,000 members.

Nottingham was to be the testing ground for the new policy. This Midland borough was a by-word for bribery and corruption, but in April 1841, by voting in unison, local Chartists had helped to break Whig control only to see the Whigs return in the summer's general election. To avoid a costly legal wrangle, the two main parties struck a deal and had agreed that when the seat again fell vacant, John Walter, the Tory candidate, should be returned unopposed. Joseph Sturge and the CSU moved to try to break this electoral pact on a comprehensive platform which included the CSU ticket, together with free trade, disestablishment and abolition of the death penalty. He had the support of some Leaguers, CSU Chartists like Henry Vincent, and on one occasion even Feargus O'Connor himself. He narrowly lost - by 1,801 to 1,885 - and he immediately set about trying to unseat Walter, claiming electoral corruption. In 1843 the result was annulled but Sturge did not stand again.

Lovett had predicted that Nottingham might be the 'Clare of England' a reference to the famous electoral victory of Daniel O'Connell in Ireland which precipitated Catholic Emancipation. Even Cobden had thought that this would mean a breakthrough. However, there is some evidence in the post-April falling sales of the *Nonconformist* that, in accepting the Six Points, Sturge and Miall may have gone too far and alienated some Nonconformist voters.

When on 27 December 1842, the CSU conference met in the Birmingham Mechanics Institute, the rioting in Staffordshire, widely perceived as fomented by the Chartists (see pages 81-82), acted as reminder of where Chartism could lead. There was also a more immediate threat: although O'Connor had been charged with seditious conspiracy, he was still at liberty and free to attend the conference. Furthermore, the potential bridge between the League and the CSU had broken down when John Bright cut his links with the CSU. Arrangements to keep out hostile Chartists had not worked and the O'Connorites were there in force. In desperation the Sturge faction had made a tacit agreement that if O'Connor was elected to the chair, they would leave the meeting.

In the event, O'Connor made no move and Sturge was elected as chairman. The discussion then turned on the agenda. Sturge's friends offered the meeting a 'Bill of Rights' which incorporated all Six Points. What they refused to accept was that this should be called 'the Charter'. In opposing this, O'Connor and Lovett temporarily were reunited; as Lovett emotionally explained, the Charter had for the last five years formed 'the basis of the present agitation in favour of the suffrage, and for seeking to obtain the legal enactment of which vast numbers have suffered imprisonment, transportation and death'.[15] A vote was taken and the meeting rejected the CSU formula by 193 to 94. Effectively the CSU was now dead. With its demise disappeared that hope of a cross-class alliance which Sturge had striven for.

His commitment to universal suffrage, based upon a Quaker sense of the value of each human soul, foundered on a word: the Charter. To the Chartists, perhaps, the loss was even greater: the potential backing of that powerful, wealthy business and industrial class from which Nonconformity drew its strength.

7 The 1842 Petition in the Commons

In the winter of 1841, a time of mounting distress, the collection of signatures for the second Chartist petition gained pace. Urging on his followers was the ubiquitous O'Connor, determined that the House should be confronted by overwhelming evidence of the people's support for constitutional reform. On 12 April, 1842, a Convention met in Dr Johnson's Tavern in Bolt Court, Fleet Street, London. In all there were only 24 delegates, a limitation imposed by lack of money. One immediate difficulty was that Sharman Crawford, an MP sympathetic to the CSU, had set an April date for the House to receive a Petition from Sturge's association. Crawford was unwilling to allow O'Connor to take precedence and on 21 April, he submitted to the House the proposal that the CSU Petition for reform be discussed in Committee. It was defeated by 226 to 67. The omens were not good for the Chartist Petition.

The day set for delivery of the Petition to the House of Commons was 2 May. On that morning a dignified cavalcade made its way to the House bearing the Petition with its 3,317,702 signatures. The illustration (see the cover of this book) gives an idea not only of the great sense of occasion, with the flags flying and the petition carried shoulder high by volunteers, but also of the well drilled order of this enormous procession. On the next day, Thomas Duncombe, the MP for Finsbury, requested that the petitioners or their representatives be heard at the bar of the House. In his speech he sought to set the Charter in its historical context while at the same time asserting that the widespread distress in the country was due in part to the lack of representation of the labouring classes themselves.

In the debate, the famous Whig historian Macaulay summed up the case against universal suffrage in these words:

1 I believe that universal suffrage would be fatal to all purposes for which government exists, and for which aristocracies and all other things exist, and that it is utterly incompatible with the very existence of civilisation. I conceive that civilisation rests upon the security of property... I will
5 assert that while property is insecure, it is not in the power of the finest soil, or of the moral and intellectual constitution of any country, to prevent the country from sinking into barbarism.[16]

Roebuck, the radical MP for Bath, spoke in favour but condemned both O'Connor as a 'malignant and cowardly demagogue' and the 'trashy doctrine' of the Charter'. By 287 to 49, the House rejected

Duncombe's motion. Hovell concludes that 'Macaulay and Roebuck had slain the great Petition'.[17] In fact, neither had done more than express the settled convictions of England's customary rulers: that the Reform Act of 1832 must be the last concession to be made to popular pressure. To go beyond this would include within the framework of the constitution classes of the population who had no 'stake in the country', that is those who were devoid of property of any kind.

8 Strikes and Disturbances

a) The Strikes

1842 was a time of almost universal distress, with short-time working and lay-offs common throughout industry. Workhouses were full to overflowing and many Poor Law authorities were compelled to grant outdoor relief to the unemployed. Wage agreements were scrapped and wages cut as employers, faced with a falling market, tried desperately to stay in profit. The ACL played on this situation stressing that, with the abolition of the Corn Laws, food would be cheaper, and that there would be fresh trade outlets and more jobs. The limitation imposed on the market by the Corn Laws, they protested, was solely responsible for the downturn in the economy. Chartists, on the other hand, were beginning to sketch out a different approach to the problem. They argued that, as workers had no property other than their labour, government had a duty to provide some protection. Enlightened employers like John Fielden and John Maxwell, in advocating compensation for workers such as the hand-loom weavers who were displaced by the new technology, were also moving in a similar direction.

In this critical year, a wave of strikes hit the industrial regions of the country. Miners went on strike in Lanarkshire, Ayrshire, South Wales and Staffordshire and textile workers in Lancashire and Yorkshire. The two most troubled areas were Lancashire and Staffordshire. The strikes have been variously described as spontaneous, or as part of a general Chartist strategy or, in Lancashire, as fomented by the Anti-Corn Law League.

Essentially the strikes were indeed spontaneous: in 1842 a general strike was no longer part of the Chartist armoury. Bitter local grievances fuelled discontent and drove workers to take action without any prior concerted plan. Wherever possible, Chartist leaders sought to capitalise on them. However, the widely-heard call for the Charter normally followed the decision to strike and should perhaps be seen as workers trying to give a political context to strikes which had their roots in hunger and distress.

As for the involvement of the League, there is sufficient evidence that, in Lancashire, League agents had been busy 'stirring up the people in the manufacturing districts in the months preceding the outbreak'.[18] Their leaders, assuming the time was ripe to widen the support for Repeal, convened a conference in Manchester of local trade union representatives and other working-class delegates, organised through the ACL ancillary, the Operative Anti-Corn Law Association. However, the meeting failed to follow the expected line and passed a resolution for the Charter 'as alone worth fighting for'. On 15 August, a follow-up meeting of the Lancashire trade unions, with representatives of 85 trades, voted to strike for the Charter. Only seven delegates opposed the motion.

Co-incidentally, the NCA had called a meeting for the next day, 16 August, the anniversary of Peterloo. The leadership, pre-occupied with the problem of break-away Chartists, was taken by surprise by the trade societies' vote. In the subsequent debates, Thomas Cooper, fresh from the disturbances in the Potteries, called for immediate action, an uprising which would force the Charter on the Tory government. Both Harney, the firebrand of 1839, and O'Connor counselled caution and the meeting finally agreed to use 'the moral strength of an united people to overcome all the physical force that tyranny can summon to its aid'. This took the form of a call for a general strike. At the conference, William Hill, the editor of the *Northern Star*, bitterly opposed this proposal, which, he argued, would inevitably lead to a confrontation between strikers and the army. The *Star* maintained the line that the strikes were part of a League plot to break government opposition to Repeal. Certainly some Leaguers welcomed the opportunity the strikes seemd to offer. John Bright, for instance, had floated the idea that all employers should shut down their factories and bring industry to a standstill with desperate workers taking to the streets. O'Connor's own position was equivocal, half-hearted in his support but unwilling to oppose the conference majority.

The 'Plug Plot', so-called because the strikers knocked the plugs out of the boilers thus bringing steam-powered production to a halt, was sporadic, beginning in Lancashire in early August. Although the trade societies had declared for the Charter - and many of their leaders were Chartists - the strikes were essentially over pay. Wages in the textile industry had been steadily reduced over the previous two years - and one aim, continually repeated, was to force a return to the wage rates of 1840. The strikers' leaders had decided that only a political solution, the Charter, would put an end to their grievances. At its height, the strike affected the hatters, bleachers, dye-workers and iron founders of Lancashire and the cotton operatives (who held out longest) together with the woollen and worsted workers of Yorkshire. Without any preparation, the 'Plug Plot' was transformed into a general strike in a major industrial area. With no central control, its leaders were unable to co-ordinate its course or negotiate collectively and consequently there was a piecemeal return to work, without any promise of improvement. By the end of August, those strikers who were still out were now concentrating on wage claims.

The Home Secretary, Sir James Graham, determined to deal with this 'mad insurrection', brought in military reinforcements and ordered the arrest of the members of the Manchester Trade Conference. By 10 August five delegates had been arrested and warrants had been issued against four others. In all 60 men, including O'Connor, were tried the following spring in Lancaster, where despite the government's hope of repressive punishment they were treated with great leniency. Although eventually 31 were convicted, a legal error in the indictment allowed them all to go free.

b) The Disturbances

In the summer of 1842, the Potteries witnessed the worst riots and attacks upon the property since the Reform Bill riots in Bristol. Discontent first surfaced in July, with a strike of the North Staffordshire miners against wage cuts, and rumbled on until the situation erupted in mid-August. Any mining strike necessarily involved the pottery workers, for the kilns could not be fired without coal. The Staffordshire Potteries was a rapidly growing industrial area, dominated by seven large companies each employing between 500 and a 1,000, with 130 smaller firms with a workforce of around 165. Pottery workers were mainly young, in part a reflection of the high mortality rate from industrial disease. The colliers were a minority, no more than 4,000, but on them depended the continuance of the entire china and earthenware production.

The district itself was squalid, with black smoke from the kilns poisoning the air and the social gulf was deep and wide 'with two classes of houses as of people - the thousands of those in the working order and the fine massy and palace-like abodes of the wealthy employers'.[19] In an area dominated by rising capitalists and the traditional ruling classes, working-class hopes were expressed in early trade unions such as the Potters' Union and later in the formation of active Chartist groups.

Chartism had had a presence there since August 1838, and had elected a delegate to the People's Convention in 1839. After the rejection of the Petition local Chartists re-formed again in 1840 under the NCA. By 1842, there were eight branches and there were more than 600 registered members. At the beginning of July, the Potteries' Chartists so reflected the national mood that they called a meeting to discuss joint action with the middle class, but they failed to find any middle-class support.

The call from the Trades Conference in Manchester for a national strike for the Charter was immediately answered in the Potteries. At a Chartist meeting, addressed by Thomas Cooper on 15 August, it was resolved 'that all labour cease until the People's Charter becomes the law of the land'. The strike began in and around Hanley and then exploded into an attack on police stations, and the houses of local worthies such as magistrates and Anglican clergy. The Reverend Benjamin Vale, the Rector of Longton, had his house set on fire and his wine cellar plundered. A member of the Stoke Board of Guardians, he 'had been advising his poverty stricken parishioners earlier in the year that they could use dock leaves to make palatable substitutes for coffee or tea'.[20]

On the following day, 16 August, a group of strikers set off towards Burslem but they were met by a troop of dragoons who opened fire, killing one and seriously wounding several more. The disturbances were now at an end and the authorities set about rounding up those held responsible.

Was it any sense a Chartist insurrection? At the subsequent trials, no evidence of any armed preparation was produced and no attempt was made on the lives of any of the local notables. Of the 276 brought to trial, possibly no more than 16 were Chartists. And yet, as Robert Fyson points out, when Vales's house was attacked there was a shout of 'Now lads we shall have the Charter', and he observes that 'this kind of "Chartism" had its foundation in a fundamental class hostility to the rich and powerful, and a readiness to take drastic acion in the hope of seeing "the world turned upside down" '.[21]

Justice was swift and severe. In Stafford, during the first two weeks of October, three judges sat in separate courts and the accused were dealt with in batches. There were no death sentences, but 56 men were sentenced to transportation and 116 men and women sent to prison for up to two years.

9 Conclusion

The year 1842 ended very much like 1839: the National Petition was rejected after a lengthy campaign which had achieved nothing, and with Chartists either in prison or facing immediate trial. But at least there had been no Newport, for Staffordshire was a riot not a failed rising. There were some differences. The movement had split apart and new groupings had appeared. Some of the old leaders such as Lovett and Vincent had fallen away, and even O'Connor after 1842 began to look at social engineering rather than political action in his plan to settle town workers on the land (see pages 87-90). 1842 is sometimes seen as the year of lost opportunities - as perhaps the only time in the history of the movement when some progress towards the eventual goal of the Charter could have been made. But was this really so?

On the face of it, despite the fragmentation reflected in the birth of Christian Chartism and Teetotal Chartism, there had seemed so many interesting possibilities. Lovett, coming out of prison a changed man, offered a self-help means of working-class advancement which assumed a pyramid of educational enterprises which would all help to forge the image of the 'respectable' working man. Was this perhaps a way forward, slow but perhaps more certain than incessant petitioning which led nowhere? If the Lovett plan had once got under way, would not Victorian England perhaps have come much sooner to a realisation of the social benefits of education and given, not only help, but eventually the accolade of the franchise? If by these means the image nursed by the middle and upper classes of a hard-drinking brawling workman could be replaced by a vision of a person more devoted to intellectual self advancement than to his pint pot, would this not have made the enfranchisement of the working class so much more acceptable?

Again, in 1842, in the ACL, Chartism faced a powerful rival, a pressure group backed by new money, industry and radical MPs. The NCA is often compared with the ACL, usually to the disparagement of the Chartists. But given the difference in power, in social status and funds, doesn't the NCA show up quite well? And again the ACL, with its free trade doctrine, was in line with the slow tide of public opinion as Peel's 1842 Budget, lowering the corn duty as well as other import tariffs, clearly showed. Against the politically respectable Adam Smith, Chartism offered Tom Paine, a thinker whose reforming ideas were anathema. With such a standard bearer, was success ever within their grasp?

It might, however, be argued that the opportunity was there with the birth of the Complete Suffrage Union. Here was a new radical base in solid Nonconformist England, wealthy and entrepreneurial. Was O'Connor's failure to seize this welcoming hand sufficient condemnation of his leadership? On the other hand, was the CSU foolish in accepting all Six Points and then drawing back finally, not on a matter of substance, but merely over the name, the Charter, under which it would campaign for reform? Is it not understandable that for Chartists this was the issue on which they could not, in conscience, yield? Such questions, however, with their implicit assumption that reform was a possibility, have to be set against the hostility of the House of Commons to the CSU petition: if the 'men of peace' could not even get a hearing, what hope would there have been for a united call from working-class Chartists and middle-class radicals?

References

1   James Epstein. *The Lion of Freedom: Feargus O'Connor and the Chartist Movement, 1832-1842* (Croom Helm, 1982), p. 226.

2   Dorothy Thompson, *The Chartists* (Temple Smith, 1984), p. 244.

3   Mark Hovell, *The Chartist Movement* (Manchester University Press, 1918), p. 86.

4   Lucy Brown, 'The Chartists and the Anti-Corn Law League' in *Chartist Studies* edited by Asa Briggs (Macmillan, 1959), p. 345.

5   Ibid, p. 345.
6   Norman McCord, *The Anti-Corn Law League* (Unwin, 1968), p. 59.
7   Alfred Plummer, *Bronterre* (George Allen and Unwin, 1971), p. 104.
8   McCord, *The Anti-Corn Law League*, p. 51.
9   Ibid, p. 102.
10 William Lovett, *Life and Struggles* (McGibbon and Kee, 1967), p. 177.
11 Hovell, *The Chartist Movement*, p. 239.
12 Plummer, *Bronterre* p. 158.
13 Epstein, *The Lion*, p. 281.
14 Joel Wiener, *William Lovett* (Manchester University Press, 1989), p. 86.
15 Lovett, *Life and Struggles* (McGibbon and Kee, 1967), p. 236.
16 Hovell, *The Chartist Movement*, p. 255.
17 Ibid, p. 258.
18 McCord, *The Anti-Corn Law League*, p. 126.
19 Robert Fyson, 'The Crisis of 1842, the Colliers' Strike and the Outbreak
    in the Potteries' in *The Chartist Experience: Studies in Working-Class
    Radicalism and Culture* edited by James Epstein and Dorothy Thompson
    (Macmillan, 1982), p. 190.
20 Ibid, p. 211.
21 Ibid, p. 210.

Answering essay questions on 'The National Charter Association and its Rivals'

I.   '1842 - a year of lost opportunities for Chartism'. Discuss.
Before beginning this question, you should decide what 'lost opportunities' you intend to discuss - and then in the first paragraph briefly refer to them to indicate what the main lines of your argument are going to be. It may be that you think that there were no genuine opportunities in 1842, that they were apparent but never real. Even if this is to be the main thrust of your essay, you could set them up as 'Aunt Sallies' to be knocked down later on. Don't spend too much time on your first paragraph. Be especially careful not to go into detail which might overload what ought to be a short, pithy introduction. It might be worthwhile to try your hand at an opening paragraph for this question.

What then would you make the key areas of your essay? Much here depends on how you view the possibility of a cross-class alliance which 1842 seemed to offer, and this discussion might perhaps form the mainstay of your answer. What judgement, for instance, would you make of the Chartist stand at the CSU conference on the question of the Charter? Again, the rejection by the House of the petitions from the Chartists and from the CSU suggests another area which it might be useful to explore. Do you think that the Lovett's 'New Move' might also be seen as a 'lost opportunity'? Did it perhaps offer a possible way forward, slow but with more likelihood of success? And should the strike movement be also also weighed in the scale?

Above all, in answering such a question, avoid a narrative approach. The higher marks go always go to the analytical rather than the narrative answer. Decide on your main themes and construct your paragraphs around them.

2. Was Chartism a national movement?
In answering this question you might also look at sections 1 and 3(a) in Chapter 4.

Draw up an essay plan which sets out the main themes of your argument. Do you intend to demonstrate that it was 'national' or to show that it was no more than a bundle of local grievances? It is, of course, open to you, to take a middle view and refer to events which seem to have no national context such as the Newport Rising or the Staffordshire riots while balancing such evidence against those aspects of the movement which are clearly national such as the NCA or the Charter itself.

If you decide that its national character provides the strongest evidence, you might wish to develop a series of related themes to support your argument. These might include the petitioning movement and the elections, the debates in the Convention, the NCA, its structure and lecturer/missionaries and the fusing of the differing grievances through the over-riding symbol of the Charter.

Section 1 in Chapter 4 gives an account of the grievances in old-established industries such as weaving and building. During the Chartist years did these local grievances ever replace the Charter as the objective of working-class action?

Source-based questions on 'The National Charter Association and its Rivals'

1. The League and the Chartists

Read the three extracts on pages 71 and 72 and answer the following questions.
a) Define briefly the following references:
　　i) 'impoverish the poor tenants' (line 36 on page 72),(2 marks)
　　ii) 'universal suffragemen'　(line 3 on page 72). (2 marks)
b) To what extent can the report in the second extract be accepted as impartial? (6 marks)
c) What is the value to the historian of the Anti-Corn Law Leaguer's speech in the first extract. (7 marks)
d) 'Sufficient common ground for a cross-class alliance never really existed'. Consider this judgement in the light of these extracts and your own knowledge. (8 marks)

Summary Diagram [*]
The National Charter Association and its Rivals

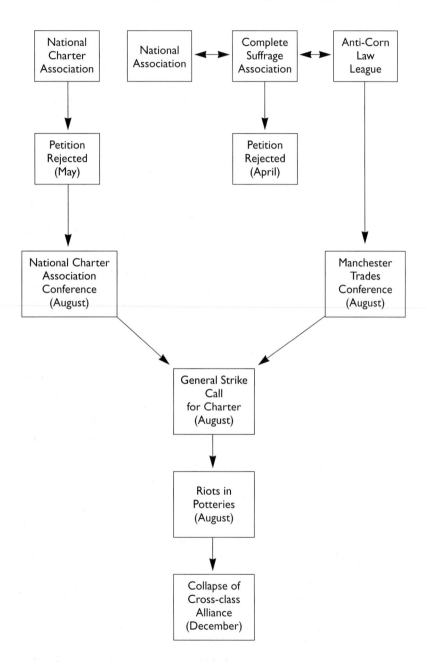

National Charter Association → Petition Rejected (May) → National Charter Association Conference (August)

National Association ↔ Complete Suffrage Association ↔ Anti-Corn Law League

Complete Suffrage Association → Petition Rejected (April)

Anti-Corn Law League → Manchester Trades Conference (August)

National Charter Association Conference (August) + Manchester Trades Conference (August) → General Strike Call for Charter (August) → Riots in Potteries (August) → Collapse of Cross-class Alliance (December)

6 The Land Plan and the Chartist Revival

With the advent of a General Election in 1847, O'Connor seized the opportunity to revive the political movement by presenting Chartist candidates at the hustings and, in the following winter as the economy ran into recession, the movement sprang once more into life. This revival of Chartism culminated in the 1848 petition and the 10 April Kennington Common meeting. This chapter considers the events surrounding that day and the political significance of the Whig government's strategy in organising so massive a defence of the capital.

However, it begins by evaluating the place in the movement's history of the Land Plan which to many of O'Connor's followers seemed to be an abandonment of the Charter and its political aims. A vocal minority of Chartists thought that at best this was an ill-advised diversion, serving only to create a new peasantry, a property-owning class who would no longer work for the Charter but entirely for themselves. To others, it was no more than a recognition that, as political action had failed, a different way would have to be found to improve the lot of the town worker. To O'Connor himself, his Plan seemed almost at times to take on a mystical significance: the answer, for which he had been searching, to the question of how best to address the desperate plight of factory hands in the new mill towns.

1 The Chartist Land Plan

After the failure of the 1842 petition, the move away from political action into a major plan for resettlement of town workers on the land looks at first sight like an aberration, due perhaps to O'Connor's 'eccentricity' rather than to a clearly thought-out policy. Yet agrarianism, the sense that the land belonged to the people and was in fact the 'people's farm', had strong roots in the English radical tradition. Malcolm Chase argues that 'the historical reality of a property system founded upon communally regulated use-rights, rather than upon absolute possession'[1] served to influence radical attitudes to the land. Folk memory of the late eighteenth and early nineteenth century enclosures still persisted - of those bad times when customary tenants had lost their right to farm their land and common land and waste lands traditionally belonging to village communities had been seized by the land-owning class, aided by Parliamentary Enclosure Acts. Once-independent villagers had become agricultural labourers or had been forced to migrate to nearby towns to look for work. These memories kept alive the conviction that the rich who made the law had seized possession of the national wealth, as the *Poor Man's Guardian* proclaimed in its columns.

Robert Owen's ideas on co-operative action led him and his

followers to the founding of ideal agrarian communities such as Harmony Hall. In London, the London Co-operative Society promoted in 1825 a land scheme remarkably similar to O'Connor's. The plan envisaged the acquisition of between 500 and 2,000 acres within 50 miles of London, based upon a share issue of £10. In the event the scheme never got off the ground but a direct descendant of the Society was the British Association for Promoting Co-operative Knowledge (BAPCK) which in 1830 issued an address signed by William Lovett and Henry Hetherington, later an influential Chartist, identifying the exclusive ownership of land by a 'a rapacious aristocracy' as responsible for placing 'the whole of the working population in the position of slaves'.[2]

In the late 1820s and in the 1830s societies interested in agrarian experiments were founded in different parts of the country, in Lancashire, in Glasgow, and in London. One of the most interesting was the Halfpenny-a-week Land Club, based on the principle of a weekly levy of halfpenny on each member's wages, using these funds to buy land. In 1835 the Club offered a cottage, a quarter of an acre of land and livestock to the next of kin of one of the Tolpuddle martyrs. Another such society was at Manea Fen in Cambridgeshire which published its own newspaper, *The Working Bee*, and proclaimed 'The land is the people's farm', a reversion to the doctrine of the early nineteenth century agrarian, Thomas Spence.

The Chartist Land Plan, then, 'can be seen as the consequence - almost the culmination - of the popular agrarian tradition' and was 'no maverick episode in the history of British working-class movements'.[3] Where it differed profoundly was in its extent: some 70,000 subscribers offered their support. For O'Connor, his proposal was part of the 'condition of England' question and a means by which the victims of the new industrialism could be plucked out of 'the manufacturing towns where their lives are embittered and shortened by excessive and ill-requited toil'.[4] Embedded in O'Connor's political and economic analysis of the ills of contemporary capitalism was a mystical attachment to 'spade husbandry', which had been shared too by Cobbett and Owen. This called for the 'culture of the land to be conducted on garden principles' for, as O'Connor affirmed, 'When I see a man with his foot upon his spade, I think I recognise the image of his God'.[5] This emphasis on the dignity of simple manual labour served to suggest to the artisan class, from which so much of O'Connor's Land Company funds were to come, a vision of an ennobling and skilled tradition quite different from the commonly-held view of the brutish life of the agricultural labourer.

Joy MacAskill traces two main reasons why O'Connor was so fervent an advocate of land settlements. Fundamental to his vision was his concept of an independent cultivator, a free man and no longer a wage slave. 'The principle of self-employment' would in turn stimulate 'the grand principle of self-reliance'. Again he envisaged smallholdings as a way of making England independent of agricultural imports, 'a desire', she writes, 'which influenced his opposition to the Anti-Corn Law League'.[6] Also, as a member of the Irish land-owning class, he may have been swayed by an idealised view of the life of his own country's peasantry.

At the Chartist conventions held in Birmingham in 1843 and in Manchester in 1844, O'Connor spoke passionately of the immediate need for land reform. At the London Convention in the following year, his advocacy led to the formation of the Chartist Land Co-operative Society on 19 May 1845. This original title was modified several times before the final name was agreed: The National Land Company.

O'Connor's initial plan was to raise the capital for buying land by selling 100,000 shares in the Land Company. These could be bought in instalments, some as little as 1/26 of the face value of the share. When an estate was bought, a ballot was taken to decide who should become the owner, with a minimum of two shares enabling the holder to enter the ballot.

In the four years in which the Land Company operated, it was surprisingly successful in raising money in nearly all parts of England, Wales and Scotland. Joy MacAskill points out that while O'Connor directed his appeal primarily to factory workers 'it is clear that he was heard by artisans of the older and smaller towns', and that 'many of his supporters could be defined more accurately as craftsmen than as factory hands'.[7]

Money for share purchase coming in small amounts could not provide sufficient capital for the purchase of the land necessary to set up shareholders as farmers. To solve this problem, therefore, O'Connor established a Land Bank to attract deposits from the trade societies which could then be loaned to the Land Company. The weakness of this plan was that the only security was the Company's land to which the shareholders could also lay claim. Furthermore the legal basis of the Land Company was never clearly defined. On discovering that the cost of registering the Company under the Joint Stock Companies Act was prohibitive, O'Connor sought the legal shelter of the Friendly Societies Act. The House of Commons responded by setting up a Select Committee which, while drawing attention to the Land Company's uncertain legal position, at the same time left it open to O'Connor to propose a way forward. O'Connor's failure to take any action led directly to the formal dissolution of the Company by Parliament in August 1851.

O'Connor's grand plan to re-settle 'the landless, helpless multitude now thronging the filthy lanes, courts and alleys of our cities' [8] failed partly through his incompetent handling of its affairs, and partly through the inability to raise sufficient capital. Throughout the short life of the scheme, support came from small savers and from the working class throughout the land, but never from the wealthy or from the landed aristocracy. It should be seen as an example of working-class self-help, based upon an idea that promised much but in the end delivered little. At a time when short-term working and seasonal unemployment were the norm, a return to the land - a reversal of the exodus forced on the countryside by enclosures - seemed to offer an alternative future. In the event, of the 70,000 shareholders only around 250 secured a small-holding, leaving the rest hungry for the land and the independence which the scheme had promised. In all, five estates were bought, a total of 1,118 acres, of which the first, Herringsgate (later named O'Connorville), was near Watford, and the others in the Worcestershire/Gloucestershire area. What may still surprise is the quality and sturdiness of the cottages built for the settlers and the presence of a substantial school building in each of the estates. Alice May Hadfield in her study of the Chartist Land Company makes the point that 'the buildings were of such good structure that cared-for ones are still in occupation, sound and strong, today'.[9] O'Connorville and its sister estates promised not only an escape from urban squalor but the hope of a life led in quiet dignity.

2 Opponents and Supporters

The debate surrounding O'Connor's ambitious venture served to keep the Chartist movement very much in the public eye. No less an observer than the most eminent political thinker of the day, John Stuart Mill, wrote warmly of the proposal in these words:

1 There is at present an experiment in progress, in more than one part of
  England, for the creation of peasant proprietors. The project is of
  Chartist origin, and it is now in full operation, near Rickmansworth, in
  Hertfordshire. Should its issue ultimately be unfavourable, the cause of
5 the failure will be in the details of the management, not in the
  Principle.[10]

However, just as it has subsequently divided historians, so O'Connor's plan divided contemporary Chartist opinion. Some like Bronterre O'Brien, already at odds with O'Connor, criticised him on theoretical grounds. In his view the land belonged to the people. It should therefore become public property (together with railways, gas and water) and then it could be leased out in small parcels to provide for the formation of a new class of small tenant farmers. In an article written in 1847, he set out his views in this way:

1 What a chain of evil follows upon the usurpation of the soil! What a
  rapid striking off of the the links of the chain would follow upon the
  nationalisation of landed property! Only prevent one set of men from
  making God's 'gift to all' their private property, and that moment you
5 open the door to unlimited improvement.[11]

Others such as Thomas Cooper simply condemned O'Connor as unfit to lead the movement. However, he still retained the support of

Harney - who had become the editor of the *Northern Star* - and of Ernest Jones, a young barrister who had joined the Chartists in the mid-1840s. Jones was essentially upper class, a member of a land-owning family, and his conversion to Chartism was to make him a life-long radical. His outstanding abilities were soon to mark him out as a possible successor to O'Connor.

3 The General Election of 1847

Although Chartist Conventions continued to meet - for instance, one was held in Leeds in August 1846 - petitioning was confined to trying to secure the release of the three Chartists sentenced after the Newport Rising. In March 1846, Parliament was presented with 249 petitions with some 1,400,000 signatures on their behalf. However, no further political move was made until the next general election, held in August 1847. This provided yet another opportunity for the Chartists to test public opinion, when 26 Chartists or Chartist-supported candidates stood for election. Some simply appeared on the hustings (see pages 73-74), made a speech setting out the Chartist programme, and then had a show of hands. Of all these candidates, the most distinguished performance was that of George Julian Harney at Tiverton, where his opponent was Lord Palmerston. For two hours, Harney criticised Palmerston's foreign policy, forcing Palmerston to give a long and detailed rebuttal. On a show of hands, Harney was the clear victor. In the subsequent poll, however, Palmerston won, with 264 votes from those few in the crowd of 3,000 who alone were entitled to vote.

In all, ten sympathisers were returned: amongst them, Sharman Crawford for Rochdale, Thomas Duncombe for Finsbury and, most importantly of all, Feargus O'Connor for Nottingham. O'Connor's opponent had been a Whig minister, Sir John Cam Hobhouse, whom he defeated by 1,257 votes to 893. When an attempt was made to over-turn this result, the NCA executive, heartened by an immediate response to their call to help, decided to organise a new petition for the Charter and to convene a Convention, charged with the duty of deciding what else should be done, if once again the petition was rejected.

4 The 1848 Petition

1848 began badly. A financial crisis in October 1847 had helped to trigger a trade depression, which was worsened by the economic effects of the revolutions in Europe. In Ireland, the failure of the potato crop, followed by famine and forced land clearances, had sharpened the demand for the Repeal of the Act of Union. One important consequence of this was that in the events of 1848 the Irish were often to make common cause with the Chartists in a joint call for the Charter and for Repeal.

It was against this background that the strategy aimed at overcoming government resistance was thrashed out. At a meeting on 11 January, Ernest Jones outlined the Chartist plan based, as before, on 'pressure from without' and confrontation.

1 We must agitate and organise! One simultaneous meeting, at one hour of the day all over the United Kingdom, to shew our organisation. One vast petition, to prove to the people themselves how strong they are in numbers. One vast procession of the men of London to present it,
5 while a Convention watches the debate and keeps piling on the pressure from without, till every town in England and Scotland rallies with the same spirit.[12]

In the run-up to the meeting of the Convention, fixed for 4 April, disturbances took place in several parts of the country, all of which were attributed to the Chartists and sufficiently tarnished the Chartist image as to create public unease. In Trafalgar Square on 6 March, an anti-tax meeting was taken over by G.W. Reynolds, a Chartist spokesman. After the meeting, the crowd failed to disperse and ran riot, smashing windows, emerging again for the following two days in the same ugly mood. The Chartist leaders tried unsuccessfully to dissociate the movement from this mob behaviour, but 'from this point on, the press refused to distinguish between rioter, revolutionary, criminal and Chartist.'[13] On the same day as the Trafalgar Square riots, the streets of Glasgow were thronged with unemployed workers, shouting 'Bread or Revolution'. And in Manchester, a crowd attacked the workhouse and the local police station. There, too, rioting persisted for a further two days. No link was ever established between the Manchester Chartists and the rioters. Indeed the disturbances arose from hunger and distress, not from Chartist agitation. As in London, the rioters were mainly youngsters; in Manchester for instance, 10 of the 14 arrested were teenagers.

Mass meetings were held throughout the country during March, one at Kennington Common with as many as 20,000 supporters. In Manchester, on 17 March, St. Patrick's Day, Irish Repealers and Chartists, led by O'Connor, took a pledge to work together for Repeal of the Act of Union and for the Charter.

The Irish link had become increasingly important in the 1840s when Daniel O'Connell turned once more to the question of Repeal. In England as well as Ireland, Repeal Associations were founded and Feargus O'Connor sought to establish an Irish-Chartist alliance, but met with stubborn resistance from the Irish leader. The emergence of Young Ireland, a militant nationalist group critical of O'Connell, led to the founding in 1847 of a new Irish organisation, the Irish Confederation. At first both Young Ireland and the Confederation were as hostile to working with the Chartists as O'Connell had been. However, the Famine bringing death and forced emigration to the

Irish people - and Feargus O'Connor's advocacy of the Irish cause in Parliament - changed Irish minds. By 10 April the Irish-Chartist alliance was in place.

The February Revolution in Paris, which replaced the unpopular Orleanist monarchy with a republic based upon universal suffrage, heightened expectations that sufficient 'pressure from without' would bring about similar fundamental changes in England and finally make the Charter the law of the land. Meetings expressing support for the new republic were held throughout the country. In London, such a meeting, with an estimated audience of some 10,000, appointed three Chartist delegates - Ernest Jones, Julian Harney and Philip M'Grath - to present a congratulatory address to the newly-elected National Assembly.

Yet when on 4 April, the 47 delegates to the Convention finally assembled, the customary divisions re-surfaced on what steps should be taken if the petition was again rejected. Some delegates argued that a new and more representative Convention, a genuine 'National Assembly,' should be convened. To Ernest Jones, however, this meant an unnecessary loss in momentum. He proposed as an alternative that the Convention should declare itself in permanent session and act as the controlling committeee, or failing that, it should stay in being until the election of a National Assembly. With considerable reluctance, the Convention delegates agreed to continue to sit until such an assembly could take over.

Central to this strategy was the assumption that the accepted policy should be based upon 'pressure from without', symbolised by mass meetings, and culminating in a great display of Chartist strength when the petition was presented ultimately to Parliament. So potent a public demonstration of popular support was precisely what the Whig government were determined to prevent. New repressive legislation was rushed through Parliament, and a long-since abandoned statute banning street processions was revived. Thousands of special consta-bles were sworn in, with the hero of Waterloo, the Duke of Wellington, in supreme command of the defence of the capital. London was on what might well be seen as a war footing. The Chartists were informed that the mass meeting on Kennington Common, arranged for 10 April, would be allowed to go ahead but that no attempt must be made to march across the Thames to the House of Commons. Any such procession trying to cross would be prevented by force. The Metropolitan police were to guard the bridges with soldiers as back-up but discreetly out of sight. On their side, the government were anxious that there should be no unneces-sary bloodshed, no repetition of 'Peterloo'.

Did the government - with the recent example of Paris in mind - anticipate a revolution in the streets? The Chartists themselves were committed to a wholly peaceful demonstration, as the poster adver-tising the meeting underlines (see page 95), and had no intention of confronting the forces of order by attempting to take the petition en masse to Westminster. Both sides wished the day to pass off peacefully and in fact both Harney and O'Brien had urged that it would be wiser to abandon the Kennington Common meeting entirely. In general, the Chartists were not given to riot - despite the press coverage after Manchester and Trafalgar Square - and they had built their hopes on following the traditional pattern of confrontation politics, with that threat of 'ulterior measures' destined to remain no more than an early example of 'gesture politics'. It would therefore seem unlikely that the government saw London as following the lead given by Paris. Indeed, as they were aware, one essential element present in Paris was absent in London: the support of the bourgeoisie. John Saville maintains that 'the distinguishing feature of the measures taken by the British government against its own radical movement, compared with the situation in Paris, was the overwhelming support given throughout the country by the middle strata of society ... from the wealthy bourgeois at the top to those referred to in the contemporary literature as the shopkeeping class'.[14]

On the morning of 10 April, from all over the capital, Chartists streamed towards Kennington Common, in readiness to proceed across the Thames to the House of Commons. The size of the crowd was variously estimated, but was at least 20,000. What happened then is a tribute to O'Connor's oratorical skills, for it was left to him to explain to the meeting that no procession could take place. In John Belchem's view, 'O'Connor served the movement well at this moment of crisis' although he 'is never given credit for the fact that some display of Chartist strength took place and that an unpropitious clash was avoided'.[15] He won the crowd over and persuaded them to disperse without any incident. It was then left to the Chartist Executive to take the petition to the Commons.

O'Connor sought to present Kennington Common as a victory for common sense and for constitutionality: in effect, the Chartists had preserved the fundamental right of meeting. It was infinitely more difficult to interpret the 'fiasco' of the Petition in a similar way. With a claimed 5,700,00 signatures, the real figure was 1,975,496. The remainder were bogus, forged or simply nonsensical such as 'Mr. Punch'. Yet to secure nearly two million signatures in so short a space of time was still a remarkable achievement.

In retrospect, the preparations made by the authorities seem excessive, verging almost on the theatrical. All the capital's principal buildings such as the General Post Office, the Guildhall and the Bank of England were barricaded (see illustration on page 96). The government's intention was to prevent the Chartists from occupying any public building which could become their headquarters. The Queen and the Court were sent to safety to Osborne, the royal palace on the Isle of Wight. As many as 4,000 police were stationed near the Thames bridges and guarding Westminster. The government had at the ready a force of more than 7,000 regular soldiers, together with more than 1,000 ex-soldiers. In support were 85,000 special constables, composed mainly of the city's middle class and of household servants, together with artisans enrolled under pressure from their employers.

In political terms, the most significant fact was the size and social composition of the contingent of special constables. There is now almost a general consensus amongst historians that this rallying of the middle classes was a propaganda triumph for the government, summed up by Edward Royle as demonstrating the government's 'ability to create a counter-demonstration of the propertied classes in the form of special constables'.[16]

CHARTIST
DEMONSTRATION !!

"PEACE and ORDER" is our MOTTO!

TO THE WORKING MEN OF LONDON.

Fellow Men,—The Press having misrepresented and vilified us and our intentions, the Demonstration Committee therefore consider it to be their duty to state that the grievances of us (the Working Classes) are deep and our demands just. We and our families are pining in misery, want, and starvation! We demand a fair day's wages for a fair day's work! We are the slaves of capital—we demand protection to our labour. We are political serfs—we demand to be free. We therefore invite all well disposed to join in our peaceful procession on

MONDAY NEXT, April 10,

As it is for the good of all that we seek to remove the evils under which we groan.

The following are the places of Meeting of THE CHARTISTS, THE TRADES, THE IRISH CONFEDERATE & REPEAL BODIES:

East Division on Stepney Green at 8 o'clock; City and Finsbury Division on Clerkenwell Green at 9 o'clock; West Division in Russell Square at 9 o'clock; and the South Division in Peckham Fields at 9 o'clock, and proceed from thence to Kennington Common.

A Chartist poster for the demonstration of 10 April, 1848

5 Conclusion

In the 1840s, the Chartist movement several times shifted direction. Parliament's stonewall refusal in 1842 to listen to the Chartist case for reform led O'Connor to experiment in social engineering and to shelve the political programme. At the time, many thought this was creating unnecessary dissension within the movement. Historians since, such as Mark Hovell, have followed the line taken by Gammage and damned the scheme. But was O'Connor no more than facing the realities of the1840s when, with the economy booming, Chartism no longer had the spur of hunger? After all, did he not yet again seize the moment and quickly rekindle the flame when, in late 1847, trade took a sudden lurch downwards? And was the Land Plan itself so out of line with a radical tradition which had flourished for so many, many years? Was its failure due entirely to mismanagement or did official hostility play a part?

One important question hangs over the resurgence of Chartism in 1848. Was the initial momentum provided by Paris and the continent, with the Chartists shaping a movement which in essence was no more than a pale imitation of the February Revolution? But although there can be no doubt that the French example did have an effect, particularly on Chartists with European links such as Julian Harney, should we not look more closely at the Irish connection, at events in Ireland and at the Irish population in England? In London, for instance, the 1841 census showed 108,548 born in Ireland. And, after all, had not working-class radicals always shown fellow-feeling for the Irish people whose menial and oppressed condition they saw as so similar to their

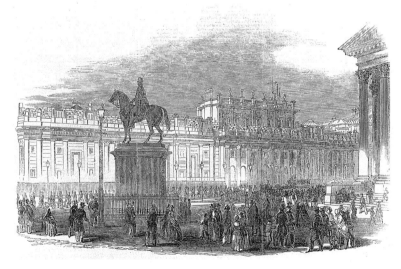

The Bank of England in a state of defence on 10 April, 1848

own? The Irish were there in force on 10 April, supporting the London Chartists, while hoping in turn that fundamental change in the electoral arrangements on the mainland would bring in its train a re-structuring of relations between Ireland and England. Should the failure of this third petition, destined to be the last, more correctly be seen as an event in Irish, as well as English, history?

The year 1848 is sometimes seen as an ignominious postscript to 1842 and 1839, a political damp squib, that a serious student of Chartism may largely ignore, with Chartists outmanoeuvred by a wise and far-seeing government who were better able to understand the country's real needs. It is compared unfavourably with Paris, Vienna or Budapest - with a barely-concealed sneer that they manage these things better across the Channel. But aren't the differences greater than the superficial resemblances? What evidence is there that O'Connor and the Chartists on that day in April had any intention of causing a revolution? And isn't the almost total lack of middle-class support the key to the situation? In Paris, whereas the middle-class took to the streets to bring down an unpopular and corrupt regime, in England from the shopocracy upwards they donned the garb of a special constable so as to deal more effectively with their working-class neighbours.

References

1 Malcolm Chase, *The People's Farm. English Radical Agrarianism 1775-1840* (Clarendon Press, 1988), p. 181.
2 Ibid, p 150.
3 Ibid, p. 174.
4 Joy MacAskill, 'The Chartist Land Plan' in *Chartist Studies* edited by Asa Briggs (Macmillan, 1962), p. 305.
5 Chase, *The People's Farm*, p. 140.
6   MacAskill, 'The Chartist Land Plan', p. 306.
7 Ibid, p. 322.
8 Ibid, p. 322.
9 Alice Mary Hadfield, *The Chartist Land Company* (David and Charles, 1970), p. 11.
10 R.G. Gammage, *History of the Chartist Movement 1837-1854* (1854) second edition 1894, reprinted with introduction by J. Saville (Frank Cass, 1969), p. 53.
11 Joe Finn, *Chartists and Chartism* (Hodder and Stoughton, 1992), pp. 72-3
12 John Belchem '1848: Feargus O'Connor and the Collapse of the Mass Platform' in *The Chartist Experience* edited by James Epstein and Dorothy Thompson, (Macmillan, 1982), p. 272.
13 Ibid, p. 279.
14 John Saville, *1848* (Cambridge University Press, 1987), p. 112.
15 Belchem, '1848', pp. 281-2.
16 Edward Royle, *Chartism* third edition (Longman, 1996), p. 45.

I. 'The Land Plan was an unhappy deviation from Chartism's main purpose'. Discuss.

This is a question which needs a clear framework if it is to be answered successfully. Was it, for instance, an 'unhappy' deviation or simply a deviation. Could a case be made out that the Land Plan may seem - at least superficially - as deviating from Chartism's main purpose yet in fact the Plan was directed at the same social ills that the Charter was intended to remove?

In planning an answer to this question - whatever approach you decide to take - decide first what the key areas are that you intend to discuss. One obvious one is that O'Connor's plan was seen by many of his fellow Chartists as a 'deviation' and divided the movement, with influential leaders such as O'Brien vigorously dissenting. Another might be to try to place the Land Plan within an established radical agrarian tradition of agricultural communities dedicated to restoring the social links that the new urban society was destroying. Yet another might be to take up the argument that O'Connor was a realist, accepting the failure both of the petitioning movement and of a cross-class alliance and looking for another way to give back dignity to those who had been dehumanised by the slum and the machine.

One key area which might justify the condemnation implicit in the quotation turns on its failure. What were the main reasons for this? Was it simply mismanagement or did the indifference of government and society at large play a part? Perhaps the visual evidence of the sturdiness of the buildings themselves could be set against this failure?

2. '1848 - a propaganda victory for the government'. Is this a fair description of the events of that year?

This question may come in different forms but essentially what is required is an assessment of the threat that Chartism represented in 1848. What points would you wish to refer to in your crucial first paragraph? If you intend to write an essay which largely agrees with the statement, obviously you would wish to refer to the preparations made by the government for the defence of the capital, with a comment on the unpredictability of crowd behaviour (in view of the manner in which previous Petitions had been presented) and the dangerous near-starvation conditions caused by the economic depression in the manufacturing districts. Clearly the shadow cast by the February Revolution in Paris should be there. As against this you might want to touch on the Chartist record of compliance with the law and in partic-ular the attitudes of the leaders in each of the previous crises. How did the Chartist leaders behave in the run-up to the submission of this Petition? And what of that middle-class support which had been so important in Paris, without which hopes of a successful coup would have been very slight? Perhaps Harney's comment is relevant here: that without the military training which the French - and other Europeans - underwent no riotous crowd offered a real threat to the State. Each of these themes offers sufficient room for a development of an argument crowned perhaps by a paragraph analysing the massive display of strength mounted by the government, with England's great war hero on display, to defeat the hordes of the enemy as he had done once before. Draw up a list of the main themes you would like to develop in the body of your essay (so as to ensure an analytical approach) and then try your hand at an opening paragraph.

Source-based questions on 'The Land Plan and the Chartist Revival'

1. O'Connor's Land Plan

Read the two extracts on page 90.

a) Define briefly the following references:
   i) 'peasant proprietor' (line 24 on page 90), (2 marks)
   ii) 'usurpation of the soil' (line 37 on page 90). (2 marks)

b) Explain the differing viewpoints expressed on the ownership of the land in the first and second extracts. (6 marks)

c) From your own knowledge, did John Stuart Mill prove to be right in identifying the probable cause of the Land Plan's failure? (7 marks)

d) 'The Chartist Land Plan was a snare and a delusion'. How far do these extracts and any other evidence known to you support this assertion? (8 marks)

Summary Diagram
The Land Plan and the Chartist Revival

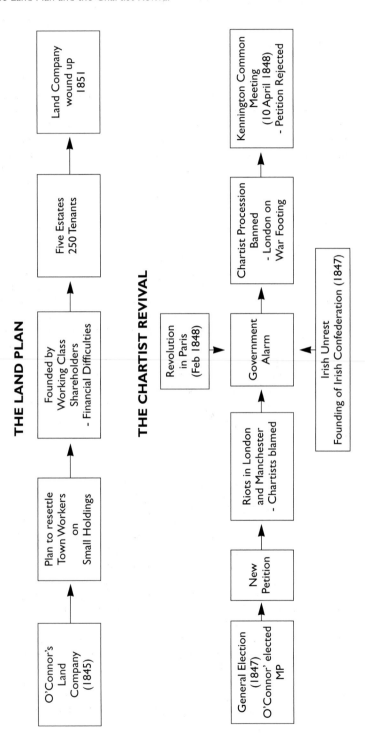

THE LAND PLAN

O'Connor's Land Company (1845) → Plan to resettle Town Workers on Small Holdings → Founded by Working Class Shareholders - Financial Difficulties → Five Estates 250 Tenants → Land Company wound up 1851

THE CHARTIST REVIVAL

General Election (1847) O'Connor' elected MP → New Petition → Riots in London and Manchester - Chartists blamed → Government Alarm ← Revolution in Paris (Feb 1848) → Chartist Procession Banned - London on War Footing → Kennington Common Meeting (10 April 1848) - Petition Rejected

Irish Unrest Founding of Irish Confederation (1847) → Government Alarm

7 The Last Decade

This chapter surveys Chartism from the failure of the 1848 petition until the ultimate demise of the movement in 1858. It begins with an assessment of the immediate results of Chartism's inability to shift middle-class England towards an understanding of the grievous distress of much of the working class in 1848. The ridicule heaped on Chartists and on the 'gross impudence' of their political ambitions stirred some to conspiracy and many others to take to the streets. The failure of these attempts and the heavy punishments inflicted on those deemed responsible put an effective end to physical force Chartism.

What took its place, as this chapter goes on to consider, was a movement very much diminished, but with leaders determined to re-define its theoretical basis. With the decline of O'Connor, leadership passed to those who were convinced that social justice must go hand-in-hand with political justice. These new men, Bronterre O'Brien, Julian Harney and Ernest Jones, were all committted socialists who tried to sustain the movement and give it both fresh impetus and a new direction. In turn, each was forced to think the unthinkable and try to negotiate a cross-class alliance, a policy which, although seemingly politically necessary, served only to alienate Chartist from Chartist. The last flag-bearer of undiluted Chartism, Ernest Jones, finally turned to this expedient in 1858. With his failure to generate working-class or even middle-class enthusiasm, he gave up the struggle and abandoned Chartism. With his withdrawal, this movement from which so many had hoped so much, disappears entirely from history.

1 The National Assembly

The events of Kennington Common and the wildly inflated Petition submitted to the House of Commons on that day, 10 April 1848, are often heralded as 'the end of Chartism'. But to Chartists such a reading ran very much contrary to their own experience as the movement continued to show a tenacious hold on life - while at the same time revealing once again its infinite capacity to fragment. The question which had been left unanswered was: what action, if any, should follow rejection of the Petition? For his part, O'Connor totally misread the situation. He was convinced that the shopocracy had now been won over and that the policy of 'pressure from without' should be abandoned. In its place, there must be an acceptance of the principle of a cross-class alliance, a common front with the middle ranks of society. But what did Chartists have to offer? Middle-class England already had the vote, the Corn Laws had been swept away by a liberalising tide - and that other great radical cause, the disestablishment of the Church of England, had never formed part of the Chartist programme. This political somersault on O'Connor's part therefore led inevitably to challenges to his leadership from within the movement - and eventually to his displacement.

Although O'Brien, Harney and Ernest Jones were all moving roughly in the same direction in formulating a socialist programme for the movement, it was the newcomer Jones, now emerging as a platform speaker in the mould of the early O'Connor, who was eventually to take over from a leader now increasingly caught up in the fortunes of the Land Company - and less and less in tune with rank and file members.

The Convention, on which so much hope had been built, dispersed without an alternative authority in place. When the National Assembly, with its French name suggesting a direct comparison with the new Assembly in Paris, met on 1 May for the first time, neither O'Connor nor Julian Harney would take part. Independently of the Chartist Assembly, O'Connor outlined his new policy, calling for a programme of social improvement which would bring the middle classes on board, working together with the Chartists for the common good. It was therefore left to Ernest Jones to propose a Memorial to the Queen as the next step, thereby utilising the traditional means of redress when Parliament failed to respond. In essence, he was advocating a petition to the Monarch. This fell well within the scope of the now-discarded confrontational tactics of the movement and which Ernest Jones now once more tried to pursue.

Within the Assembly, the issue of physical versus moral force resurfaced with the Scottish delegates in particular pushing for direct action. The NCA leadership countered by insisting that the only way to make the Charter the law of the land was by constitutional means: public meetings and lectures. In the ensuing debates, Jones's plan for a Memorial foundered and when, after a fortnight, the Assembly finally broke up, the matter was left to the Provisional Executive to pursue - in effect an abandonment of the policy. Indeed the government had already made it clear that they would not permit an approach to the Queen, notwithstanding that such a Memorial was an ancient right of her subjects.

What was patently needed was clear guidance on what, if any, the next step should be. In the absence of any direction from the centre, local Chartists were left to decide for themselves what form protest should take - and if they should now resort to the 'ultimate measure', the use of force. O'Connor's failure to take any part in the discussions at the National Assembly was an unfortunate abnegation of leadership at this critical juncture - although in defence it could be pleaded that at this time he was desperately striving to keep his Land Company afloat.

2 Riot and Revolt

a) The Provinces

From different parts of the country, reports began to reach the Home Office of drilling and para-military activity, particularly in the West Riding. At the end of May, the *Northern Star* described Halifax Chartists marching to a local meeting 'in sections, headed by an officer, wearing white blouses and black belts, the Chartist rosettes and green caps with red bands ... with music playing, banners flying, and the glittering pikes flashing in the sun'.[1] This public display of militancy was echoed in the speeches at the Convention and Assembly by their local delegate, Ernest Jones, who had made clear his conviction that, if necessary, physical force would be the 'ultimate measure'.

In nearby Bradford, Chartists had formed a National Guard and were busy drilling in preparation for future action. In Bingley, two Chartists were arrested on 20 May for drilling and were then rescued by an angry crowd. A week later, there was a more serious incident at Bradford when Chartists seized control of the town. As tension mounted, the authorities ordered in two infantry companies and units of the cavalry. On 29 May, the day following the Chartist action, the authorities moved back into the city in force, determined to arrest the leaders and to regain control. In a massive display of strength, 2,000 special constables armed with cutlasses headed an armed cavalcade into Bradford, followed by soldiers with fixed bayonets, with the cavalry in the rear. In the fighting that followed, 19 people were arrested before Bradford was brought back under its traditional authorities.

b) London

In London, tempers had been inflamed by two unrelated events: by the provocative statement from Lord John Russell, the Prime Minister, that the British people did not want the Charter and by events in Ireland where John Mitchel, the Irish Confederation leader, had been arrested. His subsequent sentence to 14 years transportation led to a series of protest meetings organised jointly by the Chartists and the metropolitan branch of the Confederation. One such took place on 28 May, when from the Theobald Wolfe Tone Club in Cock Lane, a procession set out for Trafalgar Square, estimated by *The Times* at around 50,000 strong. Demonstrations reached their climax in a protest meeting held in Bishop Bonner's Fields, in East London, where Ernest Jones was the main speaker. At the close of the meeting, a fierce fight broke out between the crowd and the police. The government reacted immediately by arresting prominent Chartists deemed to be physical force men. In all, six leaders, including Ernest Jones and the London Chartist John Vernon, were sentenced to two years imprisonment.

The trials were held shortly after the bloody street fighting in Paris and, beneath its grim shadow, the London press, radical and Tory alike, whipped up public opinion against the accused men. As A. R. Schoyen stresses, 'the evidence against Jones and Vernon could have convicted no-one in normal times but their trial early in July took place in a witch-hunting atmosphere'.[2] The Chartist leadership responded by calling for a national day of protest on Whit Monday, 12 June. In London, a meeting was arranged, once again at Bishop Bonner's Fields. The NCA Executive took the precaution of informing the government of its intention - which was to include a call for the People's Charter. The Whig ministers immediately banned all public meetings in London. The army and the special constables were put on alert. Once more, as on 10 April, public buildings were placed under armed guard.

On the day of the meeting, Peter M'Douall, the only member of the Chartist Executive remaining in London, went to Bishop Bonner's Fields to speak with the authorities there, who convinced him they would not allow any meeting to take place. He then addressed the assembled crowd and persuaded them to disperse. From the government's standpoint, they had won yet another bloodless victory: there had been no confrontation and no provocative speeches which might have incited riot and disorder.

Nevertheless, as David Goodway has established, not only did M'Douall stay near Bonner's Fields but 'it was he who took the chair in the afternoon at the Albion beershop, Bethnal Green Road, at which conspiratorial preparations for an insurrection were set in motion'.[3] The most likely time for the uprising was the weekend of 16-18 June. However, two days beforehand, on the instructions of the Chartist Executive, the meeting was abandoned, possibly because government spies had been identified as present at the initial planning meeting. This rising was to be England's 1848 Revolution. Its significance in the history of Chartism is that 'the authority of the insurrectionaries derived entirely from the Chartist Executive'.[4] The Bonner's Fields conspiracy stands out as the only known instance where the movement officially sanctioned the physical force men to take over.

3 The Last 'Uprising'

There is considerable evidence that militant Chartists, working with Irish Confederates, were intending to take to the streets in force in midsummer, on 15 August, in expectation of a nation-wide uprising. The authorities anticipated trouble particularly in Bradford and Manchester and were convinced that joint planning was going on between London and known provincial militants. In Bradford, for instance, men armed with pikes were reported to be ready and waiting only for the expected signal from the capital that the rising was beginning.

However, the first blow was struck not in London but in Ashton-under-Lyne, near Manchester, where the Irish and the Chartists took over the town, killing a policeman in the assault. As a precaution, on the night of 15 August, the authorities ordered the arrest of all the Chartist leaders in Manchester, an operation backed up by armed police and army units. The arrests continued during the whole of the next week. Without a signal from Manchester, Bradford remained quiet.

In London, as in the provinces, the Chartists worked with the Irish Confederates to mount a joint enterprise. The strong Irish presence was evidenced by the number of Irish on the planning committee - at one stage in the 'Ulterior Committee ' of nine, the sub-committee responsible for the rising , there were as many as five Irish members. The day agreed was 15 August. However, the authorities had succeeded in planting government agents in the organisation and, in the evening of that day, rounded up and arrested all the main conspirators.

Unlike the earlier conspiracy at Bonner's Fields, the Chartist Executive had taken no part in this last desperate attempt to force the acceptance of the Charter. In fact the Executive had been almost totally destroyed by the events of that summer. Of the five Executive members elected in May by the National Assembly, Ernest Jones and Peter M'Douall were in prison; O'Connor was heavily involved in trying to rescue his Land Plan; and the two remaining carried little weight in the movement. At the secondary level, there were 20 commissioners, of whom 14 had been imprisoned during that summer. As a consequence, during these critical months, Chartism lacked its charismatic national leaders, and the movement fell briefly under the control of physical force activists.

David Goodway sums up Chartism's tragic predicament as a political movement :

He observes that it was placed:

1 between pre-industrial and industrial modes of action. In the streets this
   resulted in an uneasy (and unquestionably unsuccessful) hybrid of the
   spontaneous violence of the eighteenth century riot and the pacific,
   disciplined strength of a labour movement. ... the Chartist objectives
5 were clear: the ability to hold meetings, and to move in procession.
   Chartists sought primarily for their orators to speak rather than to lead
   in revolutionary action.[5]

The political consequences of the plots, trials and disorders of the summer were disastrous for the Chartists: the very name served to conjure up 'rioter' in the public mind. For the majority in the movement opposed to violence there was a loss of faith in Chartism as the way forward. From this point onward, Chartism ceased to be a mass movement bearing the hopes of the working class for a better future.

4 O'Connor's Decline

As the sole Chartist MP, O'Connor still tried to persuade the House to give time for a full discussion of the Chartist case. In July 1849, he submitted a proposal for a motion to consider the Charter but found only 15 votes in support. A year later, a further attempt was even more humiliatingly frustrated when the House could not muster a quorum to discuss it. As a consequence of this failure, he turned once again to that wooing of the middle classes which he had so bitterly opposed in 1842, appearing on public platforms in support of Joseph Hume's Household Suffrage Association.

O'Connor's leadership of the Chartist movement was now virtually at an end. In the poll for the NCA Executive taken in 1850, he came seventh, well after Jones and Harney, who headed the poll. On the question of support for Hume's so-called 'Little Charter', the Executive was divided. Some, like Jones and Harney, were firm against any support for this watered-down programme which substituted household suffrage for universal suffrage and triennial for annual parliaments, and rejected the argument that this would lead by stages to the People's Charter. The final decision, which allowed members to decide for themselves, effectively undermined the already weakened authority of the NCA. With O'Connor's decline into madness in 1852 (he died three years later), both the old leader and to a large extent the NCA, for so long the governing body and the public voice of Chartism, no longer played any significant part in what remained of the movement

5 The Struggle for the Leadership

With O'Connor no longer at the helm, the movement needed a new leader, and with him, a possible shift away from social engineering towards a general re-assessment of its aims. At this juncture, Chartism was fortunate in having in its ranks three men who could offer a fresh interpretation and give new impetus to the movement. They were Bronterre O'Brien, Julian Harney and Ernest Jones.

a) Bronterre O'Brien

In the post-1848 downturn in O'Connor's standing, O'Brien held one strong card: he had from the outset opposed the Land Plan, first on theoretical grounds, and then as a disastrous diversion from Chartism's ultimate purpose. In a characteristic broadside in 1847, he had written:

> the strangest thing of all ... that the philanthropic Feargus O'Connor should have dragged millions of people after him in torchlight meetings, demonstrations, etc., all attended with great sacrifice of time and

money, and caused the actual ruin of thousands through imprisonment,
5 loss of employment, and expatriation, when all the while he had only to
  establish a 'National Charter Co-operative Land Society' to ensure
  social happiness for all.[6]

O'Brien found himself again in opposition to the leader when the
Chartist Convention met at the beginning of April to make the final
arrangements for the 1848 Petition. In his view, the proposed mass
meeting on Kennington Common might lead to disorder and he
refused to take part. As he failed to carry the Convention with him, on
9 April he resigned, explaining that he was now opposed to the use of
physical force and there was a clear danger that the Convention's
tactics would lead to a violent confrontation with the government.
This denial of support by one of the Convention's most powerful
speakers so angered the delegates that, led by Harney, they passed a
vote of censure on O'Brien.

O'Brien's dissenting stand did not lead to his withdrawal from the
movement - although he refused to put up for the NCA Executive -
but it effectively ruled out any likelihood that he would take over from
O'Connor. Now his main concern was to modify the traditional political theory of Chartism and to persuade the movement to link a
demand for fundamental social change to its call for political justice.

In 1849 he was a founder member of the 'National Reform League
for the Peaceful Regeneration of Society,' essentially an offshoot of
Chartism but committed to O'Brien's vision of a just society. The
League had seven stated aims, of which a comprehensive system of
social welfare, nationalisation of the land and mines, and a programe
of re-settlement of the unemployed on state-owned land were
amongst the most important.

The rupture with other Chartist leaders was quickly healed and
O'Brien was often to be found on the same platform as Jones and
Harney. He remained a committed Chartist for the rest of his life, and
a prolific writer on social themes, continually seeking to re-interpret
Chartism in the light of the changing England of his day.

b) George Julian Harney

As editor of the *Northern Star* since 1845, Harney had considerably
strengthened his position within the Chartist movement and had
become a widely-respected journalist, principally through the two or
three leading articles he wrote in his own characteristically pungent
style for each issue of the paper. He had also broadened its scope by
developing the literary section with poetry and with reviews of
contemporary novels. One other significant change was the expansion of news from abroad, a natural outcome of Harney's own interest
in European socialism. He knew both Karl Marx and Friedrich Engels
and, in fact, he was later able to persuade Engels to write for the paper

as its European correspondent.

The European dimension to Harney's radicalism and his contacts with the many European émigrés in London - where the *Star* had moved in 1844 - led to his founding a new society, the Fraternal Democrats, in the same year that he became editor. This new international association proclaimed that:

> We believe that the present state of society which permits idlers and schemers to monopolise the fruits of the earth and the productions of industry ... to be essentially unjust. The principle of universal brotherhood commands that labour and rewards should be equal.[7]

This emphasis on the unity of the international proletariat, central to Marxist socialism, was for Harney a fundamental part of his Chartist faith.

In the heady days of 1848, Harney behaved and spoke with great caution. Despite the success of the revolutionary movement in France, he had become convinced that physical force was not the answer for England. In the 1848 Convention only five of the earlier Chartist leaders had survived, of whom O'Brien, Harney and O'Connor were the best known. None of these advocated revolutionary action. In this Harney, like O'Brien, found himself out of tune with the general tone of the meetings which was set by delegates who, conscious of the distress and starvation rampant in their own districts, were in their desperation prepared to move to physical force as the 'ultimate measure'. Against this mood, Harney found himself at one with Ernest Jones, who was insisting that the next step must be the election of a National Assembly.

After the failure of the third Petition, when O'Connor came out in support of Hume's Little Charter, Harney denounced this new shift in policy as no more than a way of replacing the landed interest with the manufacturing and commercial classes. This quarrel between Harney and O'Connor - fundamentally a quarrel over the future direction of the movement - came to a head in 1850 when, in elections for the nine-member NCA Executive, four were Harney supporters, with the casting vote held by Harney himself. Under this new leadership, the Chartists went on to adopt Bronterre O'Brien's socialist programme and, by this move, had now become 'Britain's first avowedly social-democratic party - that is a party which aimed at the achievement of socialist measures through political means'.[8]

By now Harney was widely regarded as O'Connor's heir apparent. In July 1850, when Ernest Jones was released from prison, he was to add his own considerable weight to the social democratic forces within the movement represented by Harney and his supporters. However, it was also to lead to a struggle between the two men for its ultimate control. Harney himself was sensitive to the new groupings appearing in the English working class, such as the co-operative societies and, most formidably, craft unions like the Amalgamated Society of Engineers (ASE), typical of the so-called 'aristocracy of labour'. He looked to these as possible recruits in a more broadly-based movement, and as partners in the struggle for social and political justice. Ernest Jones, on the other hand, was implacably opposed to any alliance with those whom he regarded as undermining the collective interests of their own class.

In pursuit of his vision, in 1852 Harney proposed the formation of a new political party, which would take in not only the Chartist old guard, but also the trade unions, the co-operative societies and any middle-class radicals willing to accept the Six Points. At this stage, the Chartist movement was in terminal decline, with the *Northern Star* selling only 1,200 copies compared with the 21,000 in 1848, and in many parts of the country a Chartist presence was scarcely visible. The key figure of the new party was to be William Newton, the leader of the ASE, who urged that Universal Suffrage should be its platform as, in his view, a single issue campaign would have more chance of success. When Newton, faced by general apathy, backed out, Harney gave up his own attempt to re-float Chartism and withdrew from political life.

c) Ernest Jones

Ernest Jones left prison in July 1850 a convinced socialist and he quickly aligned himself with those who were working for 'Chartism under a red flag', a phrase coined in the first edition of Harney's new paper, the *Red Republican*, and which defined those within the movement who had become convinced that they must go beyond political reform to a 'social revolution'. In an article he wrote at the time he addressed in this way those whom he dubbed the 'less enlightened members of the working classes':

1 Above all, I would have them to understand, what the experience of eighteen centuries has taught us, that political power must be obtained, before social amelioration can be enjoyed; that abstinence, morality and toil, that all the efforts of united industry and intelligence are ineffectual
5 to remove the dead weight of industry, as long as the sharp sword of monopolising power is wielded by one dominating class ... THE POOR ALONE CAN WIN THE BATTLE OF THE POOR.[9]

Like Julian Harney, his fellow Chartist, Jones was in close contact with both Marx and Engels, and was very much influenced by their ideas. In his insistent refusal to ally himself with the class enemy, the 'rich' and the middle classes, Jones followed a rigid Marxist line which alienated him from those Chartists like O'Connor who were seeking support whereever it could be found. On his side, the old leader would have no truck with plans to widen the Charter into a social programme. As he explained in the *Northern Star*, 'if you mix any other "ism" with the Charter you will enlist such a host of opposition as you cannot imagine'.[10]

In the early 1850s, Ernest Jones strove to dissuade the new craft unions such as the engineers and carpenters from seeking their own economic advantage with little or no regard for the great mass of unskilled or semi-skilled workers. What was essential, he insisted, was working-class unity. It was on this point of principle that he broke with Julian Harney, his fellow socialist, when Harney moved towards a broadly-based coalition of progressive forces. From then on, the two became bitter enemies, personally as well as politically. This antagonism destroyed any hope that a united social reforming party could be constructed out of what remained of the Chartist movement.

The general absence of working-class support eventually forced Jones down that same road towards a cross-class alliance previously taken by Lovett, O'Brien, O'Connor and Harney. In the late 1850s, when Edward Miall of the *Nonconformist* came out in support of a rate-payer franchise, Ernest Jones decided to convene a Chartist Conference to work out an agreed line. This met on 8 February 1858, with 41 delegates present. There was a clear consensus on the need to work with sympathetic members of the middle classes. On its last day, Conference members held a joint meeting with middle-class radicals. The immediate consequence was the founding of the Political Reform League, with that distinguished advocate of a cross-class alliance, Joseph Sturge, as its President.

6 Conclusion

Jones's willingness to compromise Chartist principles provoked yet another split in the fast declining movement, signalled by the formation of a London-based society, the National Political Union, which challenged this new marriage of convenience. The main attacks on Jones were carried in *Reynolds Weekly Newspaper*, a radical paper which was to survive until well after the Second World War. Furthermore, some members of the Political Reform League made it clear that, for their part, they were unhappy with their close relationship with the Chartists. By the end of 1858, the League had ceased to exist. Nevertheless, the initiative taken by the Chartist Conference stimulated the founding of Manhood Suffrage associations in many parts of the country, of which the most important was the London Manhood Suffrage Demonstration Committee, organised by Jones himself. The pressure for further reform of the franchise, which was to gather pace in the 1860s, dates from this belated union of middle-class and working-class reformers.

The collapse of Jones's attempt to form a cross-class alliance marked not only his withdrawal from Chartist politics but the demise of Chartism itself. The decline in support which had begun after 1848 had left Chartism at first without a popular base and finally without a leader. As a formal movement, Chartism was now at an end, although those who called themselves Chartists were still to be found in English towns for many years to come

References

1 Dorothy Thompson, *The Chartists* (Temple Smith, 1984), p. 327.
2 A.R. Schoyen, *The Chartist Challenge* (Heinemann, 1958), p. 172.
3. David Goodway, *London Chartism 1838-1848* (Cambridge University Press, 1982), p. 87.
4 Ibid, p. 89.
5 Ibid, pp. 125-6.
6. Alfred Plummer, *Bronterre* (George Allen and Unwin, 1971), p. 187.
7 Schoyen, *The Chartist Challenge*, pp. 135-6.
8 Ibid, p. 197.
9 John Saville, *Ernest Jones: Chartist* (Lawrence and Wishart, 1952), p. 43.
10 Ibid, p. 45.

Answering essay questions on 'The Last Decade'

1. 'The 1848 Petition destroyed Chartism'. Discuss.
This question turns on the assumption that the ridicule heaped on the movement after the inflated 1848 Petition brought Chartism to a premature end. But is it true that Chartism ended then - or that its obvious decline was due to the events of 1848?

If your introductory paragraph opens up the debate, what should the key sections in your essay be? Perhaps one could be an examination of the changing nature of Chartism after 1848 and its emergence as a social democratic party under a new leader, Ernest Jones. Another might be to consider the related problem of leadership itself, the eclipse of O'Connor, the 'Lion of Freedom', and the impact of his loss on the movement. On the other hand, his leadership might be scrutinised. Did he lead the movement in the wrong direction - either in the 1840s with his Land Plan or perhaps in general? Does a comparison of the number of Chartist signatures to the two Petitions of 1842 and 1848 suggest an earlier decline?

The question allows a full discussion of the historical debate on the decline of Chartism: the perceived emerging impartiality of the State, the 'warrening' process, (see page 125) the possible penetration of individualism and the dying off of the sense of community. Each of these possibilities might be explored - together with the effect on Chartists of the State's repressive power.

Open questions such as these give an opportunity to candidates to select themes to build a persuasive argument and a highly successful answer.

2. To what extent was Chartism a revolutionary movement?
This is another example of a question where much depends on the definition of the key term, 'revolutionary'. It might be best to interpret the term in its widest connotation so that you would then be able to organise your essay around key paragraphs which examine the question in several different ways. In your introduction you could

indicate some possible intepretations.

Perhaps a natural sequence might be to look first at the moral versus physical force problem and consider how far this was 'revolutionary' rather than simply potentially riotous. Wasn't arming in self-defence a constitutional right? Even in the Newport Rising, is there any evidence that this was intentionally revolutionary? As against that, could the 15 August planned uprising be cited as genuinely revolutionary? A second line of argument might be developed around Harney's revolutionary rhetoric, inspired by the example of France, and his connection with continental socialism. Might it be useful to set this in the context of the law-abiding Conventions and the oft-repeated call for caution from the Chartist leaders? - or the care taken in setting up the NCA to keep within a very restrictive law? A third possibility might be to contrast the Chartist movement with its working-class predecessors such as the Luddites and their chosen course of action. Is it here that the real revolution took place: in replacing riot by legal processes based on novel structures such as the NCA? Again, a key and perhaps final paragraph might deal with what was essentially revolutionary in Chartism - the call for constitutional reform.

Source-based questions on 'The Last Decade'

1. New Directions
Read the two extracts on pages 108 and 109.
a) Define briefly the following references:
   i) 'idlers and schemers' (lines 7-8 on page 108), (2 marks)
   ii)'social amelioration' (line 29 on page 109). (2 marks)
b) In what significant ways does the remedy for social ills prescribed in the first extract differ from the second? (6 marks)
c) Assess the value to the historian of these documents as evidence that Chartism was continually seeking new ways forward for the movement. (7 marks)
d) Using these documents and any other evidence known to you, consider the view that neither programme offered much hope for the Chartist movement after 1848. (8 marks)

Summary Diagram
The Last Decade

THE POLITICAL MOVEMENT 1848-58

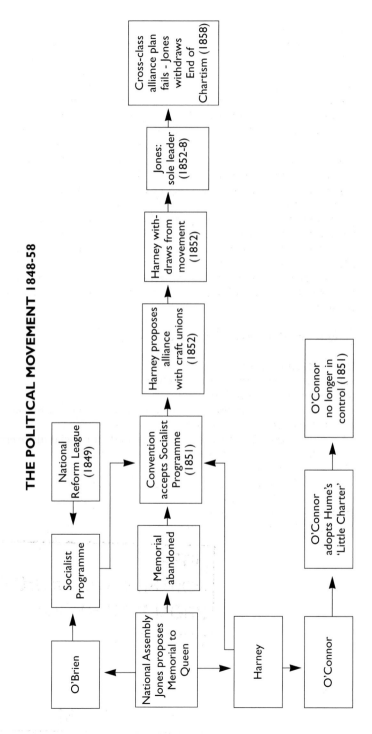

8 Conclusion: Chartism's Failure

During the lifetime of the movement, Chartism failed to achieve any of its political aims and after the rejection of the 1848 Petition rapidly ceased to be of importance to the government or to the majority of its former supporters. It might be argued that to ask 'why Chartism failed' could be countered with the question 'why did Chartism have so much success', for the ten years in which it flourished saw the rise of a movement, almost entirely working-class, which effectively raised fundamental constitutional questions in Parliament and rattled the bars of the establishment. It ran a widely-read journal of opinion and of record, organised meetings and petitions and brought the urgency of its demands to the forefront of public consciousness. Within 20 years, the 1867 Reform Act would mark the beginning of a shift towards the Chartists' main aim of universal suffrage. And in the following years, all the Six Points except annual Parliaments became part of the British Constitution. It is therefore tempting to suggest that in the long term - as well as in the short term - the Chartists were successful. But is this conclusion, attractive as it is to any sympathiser with the movement, borne out by the evidence? Did these fundamental changes owe anything at all to the Chartists.

This chapter looks first at the several explanations offered for the failure of the Chartist movement, ranging from the quality of its leaders to its inability to win friends in the powerful business class of the day. In particular, there is a discussion of the strength of forces ranged against them which continually militated against any real hope of success. This is followed by an analysis of the varied reasons which are advanced to explain the rapid decline of the movement. The concluding section suggests some of the many complex questions which any study of Chartism must necessarily involve.

1 Failure

a) Lack of Cross-class Support

Chartism failed for reasons which this study has sought to make explicit. Primarily, perhaps, it failed because, unlike the 1832 Reform Bill agitation, it was a single class campaign. If we exclude the brief flirtation in 1842 with a small group of middle-class nonconformist radicals, Chartism failed to win over any substantial section of that middle class who had benefited from 1832. They saw Chartism as a threat, a form of political levelling-up which would be to their own disadvantage if the status they had achieved were to be diluted by a mass electorate. These new and vociferous claimants were proposing changes which would produce political equality and, by implication, an increasing social equality which the class-ridden society of

Victorian England could not countenance. There must be, so ran the argument, a firm dividing line, and that should be based upon the ownership of property, which quite clearly few Chartists could lay claim to.

Furthermore, the House of Commons, to which the Chartists appealed in vain, was still dominated by the landed interest: the 1832 Reform had not seen a large influx of the industrial and commercial classes into Parliament. In the early days of Chartism, much of Attwood's energies had been directed to securing entry to the House of men like himself, successful bankers and mill-owners, so as to wrench control from the traditional and, in his view, effete governing class. To England's rulers, Chartists were seen mainly as a potential threat to public order, men and women who must be 'contained': there could be no question of conceding that there might be a case to answer.

Arrayed against the Chartists, too, were all the main sections of what might be seen as the 'managers' of Victorian society, the Church, the judiciary, the public authorities of county and town. Even in the intellectual class, there was occasional sympathy but little support. Of those Victorian novelists who depicted Chartist characters, Disraeli stood alone in his novel, *Sybil*, in creating factory girls who discuss Chartism with intelligence and insight. One book, Charles Kingsley's *Alton Locke*, had a Chartist as a central character, but the fundamental purpose of the novel was to show how misguided the search for a political solution really was: the only salvation lay in Christ.

b) Leadership

One persistent argument used to explain the failure of the movement was its tendency to fragment, broken apart, it is suggested, by constant arguments amongst its leaders. But so many other more substantial reasons can be found for the dissensions within the movement, not least the readiness of any political movement to respond to the changing currents of thought of its time. It is, after all, in the nature of politics that there should be conflicting convictions and opinions. In the Chartist years, what remained constant was the leadership of O'Connor. It was his unflagging energy, his physical strength, his oratory and to some extent his personal fortune which for so many years buoyed up the movement. Around him he recruited a team of able lieutenants - O'Brien, Harney, Vincent and later Ernest Jones - but no-one could match his skill in carrying an audience with him with an engaging mix of eloquence, good humour, invective, and a voice which compelled attention. In a pre-television age, when readiness of wit and persuasive oratory were essential to win and hold an audience, O'Connor possessed both, together with more than a dash of Irish charm.

At crucial moments in its history, O'Connor steered the movement in the direction in which he thought it should go. He held back from potentially dangerous 'ulterior measures' and moved Chartism in the 1840s towards an apparently novel remedy of ancient wrongs with his Land Plan which, although seeming to steer the movement in a totally different direction nevertheless can be seen as falling within a well-established radical tradition. In 1842 he showed a willingness to compromise with Sturge and English Nonconformity but saw clearly that such a compromise must not involve the sacrifice of the banner of the movement, the Charter itself.

As the proprietor of the *Northern Star*, he established a newspaper which, while offering weekly encouragement to Chartists throughout the land, at the same time became its official record and as a consequence the source of so much of our own knowledge of so scattered a political movement. He appointed able editors and gave them a free hand, as Harney confirmed, and wrote a regular and highly popular column himself.

Some historians, notably Mark Hovell, have offered a comparison between William Lovett and O'Connor with the balance tilted very much in favour of Lovett. On the one hand, Hovell writes:

1 the sincere, self-sacrificing, but somewhat sensitive and resentful London artisan who knew working men and shared their best aspirations, and the blustering, egotistical, intellectually and morally very unreliable Irishman, who probably had never done an honest day's work in
5 his life ... a man whose methods of agitation included hero-worship, clap-trap speeches, mass demonstrations leading to physical force ideas, and even more reckless oratory.[1]

Compare this with Edward Royle's judgment on O'Connor:

1 His was the most important and significant leadership because he was able to combine elements of camaraderie and detachment, democracy and paternalism. He built on the work of others, and with the NCA and *Northern Star* he continued to do so, but he was no mere plagiarist. The
5 sum of Chartism was greater than its parts, and that extra ingredient was O'Connor's personal magic. Men like Lovett, who would be for ever improving the working classes, were not typical of those classes, and it can be of no surprise that Lovett failed to win the enduring sympathy of more than a tiny proportion of the people. O'Connor lived closer to
10 their hearts.[2]

One issue which was always thought to have divided 'sensible' Chartists like Lovett from 'wild men' like O'Connor was that of the use of physical force. Yet although both men agreed in theory that this was the ultimate sanction, neither ever advocated it in practice. Even though, in his rhetoric, O'Connor would darkly hint at its possible use, often seeming to be pursuing a policy of brinkmanship, he drew back from openly calling for rebellion. Is it quite fair to saddle O'Connor with responsibility for the failure of Chartism without assessing the strength of the forces ranged against both him and the movement. His difficult role as the charismatic leader, the ultimate arbiter of the destiny of the movement, was played with great theatrical skill and political tact and was marked by a continuing sensitivity to the dangers which threatened Chartism and its supporters. Feargus O'Connor may be accused of misplaced optimism but surely this is part of the emotional baggage of any political leader? Ought we to weigh in the balance a leadership style innocent of autocracy together with an ability to steer the movement away from irresponsible actions which might have resulted in loss of life or mass imprisonment?

c) Strategy

Chartist strategy falls within a tradition first established with much success by the Irish Catholic Association which, under the leadership of Daniel O'Connell, forced the Tory government in 1829 to accept the necessity of Catholic Emancipation, thereby allowing Catholics into Parliament. In that crisis, a well-organised and highly disciplined movement led a traditionally unruly and discontented Irish population to confront the established authorities with a massive show of strength. This was the first step from which so much else was to follow.

In the Reform Bill crisis, a similar strategy was followed. An ostensibly entrenched and obdurate government was confronted by organised public opinion, most effectively and volubly in Attwood's Birmingham Political Union. Once more there was the implicit threat of force - just as in 1829 there had been the danger of an Irish rebellion - and in Bristol actual rioting and looting. The middle class and working class were united in demanding political reform and the Whigs skillfully destroyed that union by a limited reform which brought the middle class into the charmed circle of government. Whereas in the past, the aristocracy could be clearly identified as England's 'natural rulers', after 1832 the political balance radically altered. As Bronterre O'Brien correctly foresaw 'its effect would be to detach from the working classes a large portion of the middle ranks'.[3] Any future reform movement would now confront a realignment of the social classes. Although the majority of the population would still be excluded from the political nation, the traditional minority would be strengthened and expanded by the property-owning middle classes.

The political complacency which 1832 produced was summed up by Michael Brock in this way:

> Most of the new voters wanted, not to challenge the aristocracy, but to win recognition from it: once they had their rightful position they did not favour further adventures.[4]

Given that this was the outlook of the newly-enfranchised,

O'Connor's task in building up a a similar popular movement was profoundly more difficult than that of his predecessors. But what of that other strategy, the cross-class alliance, which at first glance might seem to have been the one great missed opportunity for the Chartists? If in 1842, they had abandoned the Charter and with it the proud title of 'Chartists', as their middle-class supporters proposed, and settled for the Charter's Six Points shorn of the symbolic banner under which they had fought for so long, would this have produced the result so desperately desired - a democratisation of the British Constitution? Parliament's summary dismissal of the Complete Suffrage Union's proposals in 1842 (see page 78) suggests the answer to this must surely be 'no'. Although 1832 had set a precedent which sooner or later would have to be followed, no further change was possible until 'democracy ceased to be one of Westminster's rude words',[5] that is until England's rulers had come to accept the necessity of a more democratic form of government.

d) Tactics

Just as the strategy deployed by the Chartists fell within an already established tradition, so for the most part did their tactics. Confrontational politicking was the mode which had brought success both in 1829 and in 1832, and this method of political action was also adopted by the Chartists. It took different forms: mass meetings with an inspirational speech from the platform; processions decked out with banners and slogans; and, of course, the final petition itself, delivered with great display to the nation's rulers. All these were designed to show the massed public opinion behind the Charter and to win over governments by demonstrating in different ways that this comprehensive reform was what the people wanted.

Beyond these public displays, there were 'ulterior measures' which formed part of the Chartists' arsenal. There were traditional forms of pressure, such as 'exclusive dealing', the boycott of unsympathetic shopkeepers. In a small community the attitude of traders would be a matter of common knowledge, and shopkeepers with a living to make might be induced to show their Chartist sympathies by practical support. Another less widely-practised form of boycott was directed at the Treasury itself by a refusal to buy goods subject to excise duty, such as beer or tea.

The 'ulterior measure' which came increasingly to be on the fringe of Chartist political action was the 'National Holiday' or general strike. In an industrial society so diverse and so fragmented, such a tactic seemed doomed to failure without the co-ordination that effective trade union organisation could bring. Mass demonstrations had something in common with industrial action yet held no risk for the participants. These were, as James Epstein comments 'celebrations of working-class solidarity and creativity' calling for a high degree of regional co-ordination. In July 1842, O'Connor himself went to such an occasion, joining a procession which made its way from Nottingham to Mansfield and then finally to Sutton-in-Ashfield. When it arrived in Sutton, the procession was reported to be around 20,000 strong. There they were greeted by a town in carnival mood. The Chartist press reported:

> Doors, windows, and walls presented hundreds of Chartist mottoes, Star portraits, flags, garlands, oak-boughs, and evergreens and roofs, windows and walls were crammed with human beings.[6]

Such community action was, at the same time, another form of political activity, a show of Chartist strength, and could be matched during the peak periods of Chartist agitation by similar displays in all the manufacturing districts where 'sons and daughters of toil' would organise celebratory teas or open air galas, with music and dance alternating with political discussion.

The ultimate 'ulterior measure', of course, was an armed rising. Although individual Chartists accepted this as the weapon of last resort, in a movement which desperately tried to stay within the law it was not widely seen as even a possible threat. If citizens took up arms, so the argument ran amongst the 'physical force' men, working-class soldiers would fraternise with their fellows in the ranks of the Chartists. Yet such confidence in class loyalty was totally misplaced, as the tragedy of Newport clearly demonstrated. Fortunately, theory was not otherwise put to the test - although London in 1848 provided evidence that Chartist supporters were willing to risk life and limb to secure the Charter. Perhaps Harney's insightful comparison between England and the continent is worth considering here: that the absence of conscription and the consequential lack of military training this side of the Channel is an important factor in considering the Chartist failure to take up arms. This would mean that British revolutionaries, unlike their French counterparts, would have neither the predisposition nor the necessary skill to take to the streets.

The terms 'moral force' and 'physical force' were coined by R.G. Gammage, the Chartist historian, to define what he saw as two conflicting wings of the movement. For many years, discussion has focussed on these as radically opposed courses of action open to the Chartists - with often the unspoken implication that if only the Chartists had toed the 'moral force' line they would have fared much better. But is this view really tenable? Perhaps the very distinction between the two is artificial. It was widely accepted in early Victorian England that a free-born Englishman had the right to bear arms and to use them in self-defence - a view still held even today in a country like the United States with its strong English common law tradition. Lovett, so long held up as the great exponent of 'moral force', had in his pre-Convention days even gone beyond this essentially defensive position to talk of the need for aggressive action for political ends.

More important, however, is the question of what chance 'moral force' had of succeeding. A comparison with the Anti-Corn Law League may be helpful in considering this question. The ACL was essentially a moral force campaign, well funded and well led with extensive middle-class support, arguing a case which had the backing of wealthy manufacturers who saw it as bringing a boost to their industries by making exports easier to corn-importing countries. Nevertheless it was not the strength or justice of their campaign which won the day, but the conversion of Peel and the inexorable logic of the free trade philosophy which brought about Repeal. On their side, nothing the Chartists were pressing for chimed in with the mood of the times now that all those with a 'stake in the country' had had their political demands satisfied by the 1832 Act. Whatever considered arguments or moral force the Chartists brought to bear seem unlikely to have been able to shift those classes who now held a monopoly of political power.

2 The Forces Against the Chartists

a) The State and the Chartists

Throughout the Chartist period, relations between the State and the movement were always marked by mutual suspicion. 'Peterloo' (see pages 10-11) stood in working-class minds as evidence of what they might expect from a hostile government. Ministers, on their side, were also determined that there would be no new massacre and that the sabre-wielding Yeomanry should never again be let loose to cut and slash a defenceless crowd. However, except on that one point, the attitudes of governments were never constant: Whigs, for instance, were traditionally less interventionist than Tories. Even between different Whig administrations there were profound differences, with Lord John Russell as Home Secretary far more reluctant to take repressive action than Lord Melbourne, his fellow Whig.

But even Russell's own record was patchy. At the onset of the movement, as Home Secretary, he readily tolerated the mass meetings held to elect delegates to the Convention. Indeed, in October 1838, as F.C. Mather comments, 'he boasted of his refusal to put down Chartist meetings and of his reluctance to sanction secret service expenditure'.[7] Yet when in the early months of 1839, Russell was once more at the Home Office, despite his proclaimed liberalism, he had the mail of Convention delegates secretly inspected. But he refused to support moves to disarm the Chartists or to allow the formation of armed vigilante groups.

Again, faced with growing unrest in the run-up to the July submission of the Petition to Parliament, Russell's attitude hardened. He moved with increasing firmness against the Chartists, arresting Henry Vincent, one of their best speakers, banning drilling and permitting the arming of citizen defence forces. The difficulties of the government were compounded by the unsatisfactory state of the law. The Bill of Rights of 1689 had proclaimed that 'all the subjects which are Protestants may have arms for their defence, according to their condition and as allowed by law'. Therefore any seizure of arms required the authorities to establish that the arms were intended to be used to disturb the peace - in itself no easy task. In 1848, Russell reverted to his earlier relaxed approach. There was no attempt to ban public meetings, and processions were permitted throughout London. In fact, Russell at first had been willing to allow a Chartist procession to bring the Petition to the House itself. All the measures taken on that day were defensive rather than offensive.

In contrast, the Conservatives, in office during the 1842 campaign, took immediate preventive action when faced with the strikes of that summer. With the advantage of the new rail network, Sir James Graham, the Home Secretary, transferred large bodies of troops to the strike-bound districts, banned all mass meetings, and arrested the members of the Manchester Trades Conference. Determined to root out all trouble-makers, he tried - unsuccessfully - to have all 60 defendants (including O'Connor) charged with high treason.

During the Chartist decade, the forces available to the State were very much improved. Initially in 1839, there was no effective local police force, and the maintenance of public order depended in the last resort on the army. Fortunately for all concerned, the officer commanding the Northern District was General Napier, a humane and civilised man, himself sympathetic to the Chartists. In these difficult months, he used his influence to warn the Chartists against the use of force and at the same time curbed the enthusiasm of the local JPs eager to break up Chartist meetings. In the subsequent crises, the 1839 Rural Police Bill gave local authorities the right to determine whether the cost to the ratepayer of raising a local force could be justified. However weak, this Act ensured that in 1842 and in 1848 some towns at least would have their own local police force.

b) The Judiciary and the Law

The Chartists were confronted by a judicial system which was heavily weighted against them. The judges who tried them were uniformly from upper middle-class backgrounds and with little understanding of, or sympathy with, working-class defendants. The jury consisted of 12 members of the shopkeeping class who, in the words of Holdsworth, the legal historian, 'adopted their usual attitude of deference to judges who were able and impartial', a statement which in itself reflects the hierarchical values of Victorian society.[8]

In the Chartist trials, the presiding judge would often deliver a political speech outlining the advantages of a social system which conferred benefits on so many. Two examples will give the flavour of such addresses. Baron Alderson at Chester Assizes in 1848 observed that:

1 the people would readily be brought to understand that the accumula-
   tion of capital in the manufacturing districts was a blessing to the
   workmen ... then also the poor would more readily learn that the
   possession of large estates, not used merely for the purpose of luxury
5 and private gratification, was a blessing to the poor, in promoting the
   establishment of schools, churches and other institutions calculated to
   ameliorate our social conditions.[9]

At the trial of Ernest Jones, Sir Thomas Wilde developed a similar theme:

Nothing can be more delusive, nothing more unjust, than to be telling
the poor man that the rich are robbing him. The fine horses, the fine
parks and the splendid equipages, have been the result of labour of days
and nights and of frugality.[10]

Chartists did not share quite the same complacent view of English society and its distribution of wealth as a Newcastle woman Chartist made clear in an issue of the *Northern Star*:

1 We have searched and found that the cause of these evils is the government of the country being in the hands of a few of the upper and middle
   classes, while the working men who form the millions, the strength and
   wealth of the country, are left without the pale of the Constitution, their
5 wishes never consulted, and their interests sacrificed by the ruling
   factions, who have created useless officers and enormous salaries for
   their own aggrandisement. We tell the wealthy, the high and mighty ones
   of the land, our kindred shall be free. We tell their lordly dames we love
   our husbands as well as they love theirs, that our homes shall be no
10 longer destitute of comfort, that in sickness, want and old age, we will
   not be separated from them, that our children are near and dear to us
   and shall not be torn from us.[11]

After each upsurge of Chartist activity, great numbers of Chartists were arrested and brought to trial. In 1839, for instance, 543 Chartists were sent to prison. One particular injustice of the legal system turned on the implications of bail or the financial 'sureties' imposed on a released prisoner which were intended to act as guarantees of good behaviour. Poorer prisoners often had great difficulty in finding the money necessary to secure release on bail. In a case in Bradford in 1848, of 58 prisoners only nine could meet the bail requirements. Again, if on release, too large a sum (in a working man's terms) had been fixed as surety - forfeit if the ex-prisoner offended again - the inability of a prisoner due for release to raise the necessary money would mean that he would stay in jail until he had served the extra period of time which the surety would have covered.

The Chartist movement faced an unsympathetic Parliament, a

hostile Bench and a middle class firmly entrenched in its complacent conviction that, compared with the unfortunate foreigner, Englishmen were living in a land where there existed ample opportunity for all to achieve status and wealth. In 1848, the middle class in London rallied in great numbers to the call to defend the capital. A similar response marked the provincial cities. There the special constable, in hundreds or even thousands, turned out in support of the army and the police. This almost universal defence of the *status quo* was the defining factor in any comparison between England and France, where at times the middle class manned the barricades alongside the French worker. The difference between the two societies, *The Times* pointed out in an editorial in 1848, rested on the fact that 'the people feel under the existing state of things they have a voice in the government of the country, and can utter that voice with effect'. Clearly 'people,' in the magisterial view of the national newspaper, rightly excluded all those like women and Chartists who had no audible 'voice in the government'.

3 Decline

The Chartist movement was based on the conviction that no general improvements in working-class life could take place without the vote. When changes for the better came without enfranchisement, a recent historical analysis suggests, working-class perceptions of the nature of the Victorian state were altered, with a consequent weakening of their case.

This general argument is advanced by Gareth Steadman Jones in this way:

> Chartism disintegrated in the early 1840s. Chartist decline was not initially the result of prosperity and economic stabilisation. For it effectively preceded them. Its rise and fall is to be related in the first instance...to the changing nature of the State.[12]

Chartists viewed the State as an instrument of oppression, responsible for 'class legislation'. This view was necessarily challenged when, in the 1840s, the State behaved in a manner more even-handed, passing legislation which ran counter to the class interests of powerful lobbies. The most obvious example of such legislation was the Repeal in 1846 of the Corn Laws in which Robert Peel bitterly offended the farmers and the landowners by extending free trade to include corn. But even before that, the process by which the State intervened to achieve a balance of interests had begun with Mines Act (1842) which had ended women's and children's labour underground, and the Factory Act (1844) limiting the hours of work of women and children in the textile mills. Further steps were taken to improve working-class life with the abolition of the hated Poor Law Commission in 1847, the passing of the 'Ten Hour' Act in 1847 and the first Public Health legislation of 1848.

The 1847 Factory Act marked the beginning of a fixed ten-hour day for mill-workers and the 1848 Public Health Act, by creating a General Board of Health (and where local authorities thought fit, corresponding Local Boards of Health), made a slow start in dealing with the health and sanitation problems of Britain's disease-ridden cities.

The question may well be asked: how far did Chartist agitation help to induce an otherwise remote administration to concern itself with what may loosely be called 'social legislation'? Certainly individual politicians such as Robert Peel, great landowners like Lord Ashley, and gifted administrators such as Edwin Chadwick were all concerned with the 'condition of England' question. In the minds of such men, there was a conviction that fundamental change was needed and each was responsible for significant reforms affecting the lives of Chartist supporters: Peel for Corn Law Repeal, Ashley in Factory Reform and Chadwick not only the New Poor Law but in public health . However, there is some evidence of a more accommodating tone, a less aggressive stance, on the part of government and the governing classes as a whole which may have arisen from the public airing of working-class grievances which Chartism produced. Again, from the standpoint of the beneficiaries, did these new, seemingly-impartial measures, affect working-class attitudes sufficiently to persuade them, as Gareth Steadman Jones argues, to turn aside from an agitation which had produced no tangible results at all?

A further refinement of this thesis turns on the language used by Chartists in their campaigns. In Gareth Steadman Jones's view, the political analysis deployed by the Chartists had been inherited from a radical tradition developed in a quite different society where power and privilege were in the hands of an aristocratic minority. In that radical tradition, the defects of English society were seen to be due to the monopoly of political power enjoyed by the few. With the widening of the franchise in 1832, and the subsequent Whig reforms, the Chartists came to see the middle class as going over to the enemy; and no longer part of the 'people'. Nevertheless, Chartists failed to alter their political language in accordance with this fundamental change and still fell back on what was essentially an eighteenth-century political analysis. They were unable to develop a political vocabulary which confronted the new situation reflected in the 1832 Act and the social and economic changes brought about by the rapid expansion of manufacturing industry. A radical vocabulary which served to unite the middle and working classes was still being used in the 1830s and 1840 when clearly the middle class saw their interests as quite distinct from the 'people', i.e. the working class. A passage from Julian Harney may serve to illustrate this point. As late as 1850, he was still using the individualist assumptions of Natural Rights:

THE LAND BELONGS TO ALL and the natural right of all is superior to the falsely asserted rights of conquest and purchase.[13]

This continuing use of a radical ideology, runs the argument, made it so much easier for Chartism to merge with the new Liberalism of the 1860s.

A quite different explanation for Chartism's decline is suggested by E.P. Thompson:

> For the workers, having failed to overthrow capitalist society, proceed to warren it from end to end.[14]

'Warrening' is the term coined by Thompson to describe the growth of alternative working-class institutions, such as the Friendly Societies, many of which pre-dated Chartism. The Friendly Society was the fundamental self-help support of working-class life. By 1847 the official figures record more than 10,000 societies and a membership of slightly less than 800,000, although it is likely that the actual membership was very much more. Such penetration by a savings movement suggests a concern for a personal safety net which conflicts with middle-class perceptions of the profligate working class. On the other hand, it may also be used to support an argument which looks to a permeation of middle-class values as one reason for the decline of Chartism.

Another aspect of the 'warrening' process which had begun long before Chartism was the growth of trade unions. Once the attempt to form a comprehensive union, such as the Grand National Consolidated Trades Union (see pages 16-17) had been abandoned, trade associations developed which were limited in scope and function, concerned only with working conditions and wages. One other important development was the growth of the co-operative movement. There had been early Owenite attempts at co-operative stores but the first continuously successful store was that founded in 1844 by Rochdale Chartists, the 'Rochdale Pioneers'. An answer to company shops and a means of providing cheap supplies to working-class customers, the co-operative movement offered the further advantages of community participation (through the necessity of becoming a member) and of a savings scheme by offering a five per cent dividend on purchases, the famous 'divvy'.

Dorothy Thompson suggests a further reason for its decline, and indeed for the absence of an alternative political movement rooted in the local community in a similar way. She sees the growth of the large city as bringing with it the end of the small community where neighbour knew neighbour and where control could be 'exercised over shopkeepers, constables, schoolteachers, local preachers and even Poor Law Guardians. Organisation moved from the home, the inn and the street to the large workshop and the trades club.'[15] Chartism had local roots which withered as the city grew.

4 The Coming of Reform

During the late 1860s political reform associations sprang up in many British towns, some led by old Chartists, others (such as the Reform Union in Manchester) an offspring of the old Anti-Corn Law League. Of these new groups, the powerful Reform League was essentially an example of that cross-class alliance sought in 1842, with a barrister as president and a trade unionist as secretary. Extra-parliamentary pressure built up, culminating in the famous Hyde Park meeting of the Reform League on 6 May 1867, held despite a government ban, and the 1867 Reform Act seems on the surface to be its direct consequence. However, the 1867 Act was essentially the result of politicking by the two traditional parties. Disraeli's eventual bill should be seen as the work of an astute politician anxious to find a new constituency for a party excluded for so long from power, rather than as concession to the reform groups outside the House, clamouring for an extension of the franchise.

This was the second step from which all else was to follow. The 1866 electorate of around one million was practically doubled by the 1867 Reform Act, which not only established the principle of household suffrage but also gave the vote to lodgers. The subsequent reform of 1884 threw the net even wider by destroying the hold of the great families on the counties and enfranchised the agricultural labourers. The political democracy for which the Chartists had fought for so long had now finally been achieved - although based on male and not on universal suffrage. Within this new political society working-class voters were eventually to turn to the Liberal Party in strength, an alignment which culminated in the election in industrial constituencies of working-class Liberal MPs.

The militancy which marked the Chartists was lost in the mainstream Lib-Lab pact which from 1869 until the formation of the Labour Representation Committee in 1900 supported the Liberal Party. Only within small parties such as the Independent Labour Party or the Social Democratic Federation did it briefly survive. It is perhaps one of the ironies of history that that political urgency driving Chartism was only to re-surface in another single-sex campaign, the women's suffrage movement .

5 Conclusion

Although the Chartist movement as a significant political force lasted no more than ten years, political discontent had been the cause of governmental disquiet since the beginning of the century. Successive governments had been confronted by orators, pamphleteers and crusading political associations at many other times before. The capacity for the committed to organise and agitate had been most marked in the way in which popular opinion had been marshalled to bring about the emancipation of the slaves in the British Empire in 1833. Did Chartism represent yet another example of a marshalling of public opinion, another pressure group pushing for much needed change? Is it perhaps useful to ask if the two movements had anything in common? Does one obvious similarity lie in the extent of middle-class support for both - seen in the role of the BPU in the first stage of the movement? But aren't the contrasts even more striking? The abolitionists not only had the backing of several influential MPs but they also had the wind behind them in that the economic case for emancipation had come to be widely accepted: the new economic liberalism advocated individual freedom and the replacement of the dependency of the slave by the independence of the free man.

And where was the phalanx of MPs in support of the Chartists? And most importantly, what economic gain was to be made by granting political equality to the mass of the people? Such a fundamental shift in the basis of society could more readily be seen as a danger to the property-owning classes. Isn't a closer parallel to emancipation to be found in the 'success' of the Anti-Corn Law League? A strong Parliamentary lobby with Nonconformist backing, and most of all, a cause which reflected the dominant economic philosophy, expounded by the breed of thrusting capitalist entrepreneurs symbolised by Manchester itself.

Did Chartism comprise not only a threat to the *status quo* but also a continuing threat to public order? The confrontational menace of its leaders fed the public's fear, particularly the menace in their oft-repeated slogan: 'Peaceably if we may, forcibly if we must'. The earlier campaigns in the manufacturing districts against the New Poor Law had helped fuel that fear as they had often spilled over into lawlessness. Nevertheless Chartism did not, in general, fall back on what has been termed 'folk violence'. The question posed by Dorothy Thompson is why in the late 1830s 'the British workers responded to hunger by forming a nation-wide movement around a political programme instead of by more traditional means of protest such as food rioting, arson, begging, poaching or praying.'[15] Again, rhetoric apart, wasn't the general style of the movement more in the nature of a rational discourse with the rest of society, in particular with those nearest to them on the social ladder, the middle class?

That this political style broke down in Newport is clearly evident, although what happened and why it happened are matters still very much open to debate. Again, after Newport, did plans exist for a national rising to rescue Frost from the scaffold? There is some evidence of an extensive network of militants awaiting a signal that never came, for O'Connor continually urged caution. In Bradford, on 26 and 27 January 1840, a small-scale rising took place but the commutation on 1 February of Frost's sentence ended the likelihood of any further rising. After 1840, with the formation of the NCA, did Chartism undergo a change of heart, with the constitutional route to political reform becoming the only acceptable way? In fact, was rebellion ever considered a serious alternative for the majority of Chartists to the traditional means of securing redress?

How far did the idea of class sustain the Chartist movement? Were Chartists seized with a sense of class unity defining them as a separate class in society? To the England of the time, the notion of class was a novel one. To Tories such as Peel, it was anathema and had no place in his political vocabulary. The traditional model of society to which he and other like-minded politicians subscribed was based on differing ranks and orders, with the old Unreformed Parliament as representative of all. After 1832, such an interpretation could no longer easily be held as the new property qualification, the famous Ten Pound Householder franchise, enacted a clear dividing line in society.

In this more clearly defined world, middle-class radicals like Thomas Attwood tried to cross the new boundary by seeking to create a union of the 'industrious classes' pitted against the 'non-producers', government and aristocracy. This attempt did not survive the 1839 Convention; after this, Chartism not only lost its middle-class element but re-organised itself around a newly-emerging concept of class which set working-class interests firmly against those of manufacturers and non-producers alike. Was the Complete Suffrage Union in 1842 a fresh attempt to follow Attwood's path? And was the Anti-Corn Law League's wooing of working-class support another way of yoking together the 'industrious classes' against those 'who toil not neither do they spin' - the landed aristocracy?

All these attempts to forge a common bond between classes with radically-opposed interests were in vain. Working-class Chartists were unable to find a community of interests between themselves as 'a despised caste' and those who held not only political power but also enjoyed 'the gladness of plenty.'[16] Does this failure suggest an important truth about Chartism: that it served to create a sense of working-class unity and thereby helped to transform the 'working classes' into the 'working class'?

Victorian society was built on 'deference', on a ready acceptance of social differences and a willingness to defer to 'one's betters'. Chartists challenged these comfortable assumptions by asserting a sense of their own worth as the sole producers of the nation's wealth. One offshoot of this challenge was a wish that their children should not be inducted into a system which would assign them a permanently subordinate role in society, drilled to accept the established social codes and their place at the base of the social pyramid. Their vision was of an educational system, not only free and universal, but springing from the local community. Should the system of education for the working class which emerged be seen as yet further evidence of the extent of Chartist 'failure' - a system not only remotely controlled but marked by its insistence on established authority framed, perhaps, to instill social discipline into the lower orders?

Some veteran Chartists passed smoothly over into the Liberal camp and jettisoned all their erstwhile radical views. E.P. Thompson cites a dinner of old comrades, held in 1885 at a Halifax Temperance hotel, where a vote of thanks was moved to Mr Gladstone for 'passing into law those principles which we have endeavoured during a long life to enjoy.' This motion was seconded by George Webber, once a physical force militant. It was recorded 'that the majority of those attending the meeting have become men of business and in some cases employers of labour', evidence, as the reporter noted, of the virtues of 'economy, industry and temperance.'[17] But is this not only evidence of the successful penetration into the working class of the middle-class Liberal ethos but also of something more - of a potential ability hitherto unrecognised and unused by society?

As we have seen, there are many possible explanations why Chartism withered and died after 1848. In particular, reforms fundamentally affecting working-class life, on the evidence of the Mines and Factory Acts, for the first time seemed possible without the franchise. The very need for political action was no longer quite so obvious. However, the cyclical depressions which up to 1850 had dogged British industry did not entirely disappear - 1858 and 1866 were both years of economic depression. And in eight of the years between 1851 and 1864, wages stood at around the level of 1850. Improvement came later and by the end of the century working-class incomes in real terms had improved by as much as 50 per cent. Perhaps not too much should be made of this 'improvement' for working-class families in the industrial towns still lived mainly in sub-standard housing. Is there also a case to be made out for working-class acceptance of the necessity for self-advancement which was the hallmark of middle-class England? Did the working class come to recognise that 'it was the bounden duty of every citizen to better his social status', as Beatrice Webb claimed?[18] Did the sense of community reflected in Chartism give way to a commitment to self-improvement most evident in the new-style trade unions such as the Amalgamated Society of Engineers which were concerned with sectional rather than class interests and committed to improvements for union members rather than to the working class as a whole?

Any study of the Chartist movement must of necessity leave many such questions unanswered for no full account of the movement or of its implications for working-class Britain as yet exists. Much work has still to be done. Therefore answers must be tentative. What is certain, however, is our enduring interest in a movement which gave purpose and shape to the lives of so many working-class people.

References

1   Mark Hovell, *The Chartist Movement* (Manchester University Press, 1918), p. 67.
2   Edward Royle, *Chartism*, third edition (Longman, 1996) pp. 61-2.
3   E.P. Thompson, *The Making of the English Working Class* (Penguin, 1974), p. 903.
4   Michael Brock, *The Great Reform Act* (Gregg Revivals, 1973) p. 319.
5   Eric J. Evans, *The Forging of the Modern State* (Longman, 1983), p. 218.
6   James Epstein, 'Some Organisational and Cultural Aspects of the Chartist Movement in Nottingham' in *The Chartist Experience: Studies in Working-Class Radicalism and Culture 1830-60* edited by James Epstein and Dorothy Thompson (Macmillan, 1982), p. 249.
7   F. C. Mather, 'The Government and the Chartists' in *Chartist Studies* edited by Asa Briggs (Macmillan, 1959), p. 376.
8.   John Saville, *1848. The British State and the Chartist Movement* (Cambridge University Press, 1987), p. 167.
9   Ibid, p. 176.
10   Ibid, p.178.
11   Gareth Steadman Jones, 'The Language of Chartism' in *The Chartist Experience*, p. 52.
12   Ibid, p. 33.
13   Saville, 1848, p. 208.
14.   Dorothy Thompson, *The Chartists* (Temple Smith, 1984) p. 338.
15   Dorothy Thompson, *The Early Chartists* (Macmillan, 1971), p. 12.
16   Ibid, p. 129.
17   E.P. Thompson, 'Homage to Tom Maguire' in *Essays in Labour History* edited by Asa Briggs and John Saville (Macmillan, 1960), p. 282.
18   Asa Briggs, ' The Language of "Class" in Early Nineteenth Century England ' in *Essays in Labour History*, p. 71.

Answering essay questions on 'Conclusion: Chartism's Failure'

Essay questions on the failure of Chartism tend to be of two main types. They may focus on the leadership of the movement or on the general improvement in working-class conditions after the 1840s.

   These are typical questions.

1. 'A movement cursed with poor leadership'. How far is this true of Chartism?

2. 'The improvement in the British economy and in the quality of working-class life made Chartism increasingly irrelevant'. Do you agree with this judgement?

Both these questions have in common the assumption that Chartism could have succeeded but for ... It is therefore worthwhile to ask yourself, before beginning to answer questions of this kind, whether you agree with this assumption. In the first paragraph, do set out the general outlines of your argument. For instance, in answering question 1, decide whether O'Connor's leadership is wholly or partly to blame. If you think there are other factors which should be taken into account, such as the lack of cross-class support or the hostility of property-owning Britain, you should briefly refer to them in your opening paragraph and of course develop these arguments more fully in separate paragraphs. Do also bear in mind that if you are asked 'how far' or 'to what extent' you must make clear the extent of your agreement or disagreement. And that there can be no definite 'answer' but only a carefully developed hypothesis based on your own knowledge and understanding.

On the other hand, question 2 takes up the broader question of the virtual disappearance of Chartism after 1848, apart from the rump of the movement. You might like to consider how far, if at all, the ridicule poured on the movement after the 1848 Petition affected its support in the country. In any case, as in all questions, have a clear essay plan in mind to help you decide what the main outlines of your argument should be. One line might be to consider the relationship between the expanding economy of the second half of the century (although wages were often no higher) and the cyclical depressions and the peaks of the movement.

Another might be to discuss the actual improvements in working-class life brought about by social reforms such as successive Factory Acts. Again, you might like to examine working-class self-help movements such as the co-operatives, the Friendly Societies, the Building Societies and trade unions as offering an alternative route to improvement. Perhaps also the simple acceptance of the impossibility of making progress on the political front played some part in the quiescence of the working class after 1848. Another line of argument might turn on the power of the State reflected in the numbers imprisoned and, as a consequence, a possible unwillingness to run such risks against entrenched public opinion and government.

Source-based questions on 'Conclusion: Chartism's Failure'

1. Two Analyses of English Society
Read the three extracts on pages 122 and 124.
a) Define briefly the following references:
   i) 'without the pale of the Constitution' (line 22 on page 122), (2 marks)
   ii) 'falsely asserted rights' (line 46 on page 124). (2 marks)
b) Does the second extract effectively sum up the Chartist case? (6 marks)
c) How far do you think that the first extract reflects a widely-held view of the workings of mid-nineteenth century society? (7 marks)
d) 'The property-owning classes had good reason to fear the Chartists'. Do these extracts and your own knowledge support this assertion? (8 marks)

Summary Diagram
Conclusion: Chartism's Failure

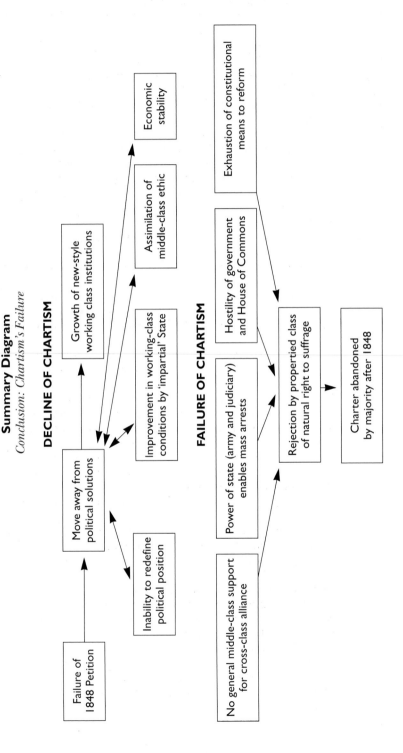

DECLINE OF CHARTISM

Failure of 1848 Petition

Move away from political solutions

Inability to redefine political position

Growth of new-style working class institutions

Improvement in working-class conditions by 'impartial' State

Assimilation of middle-class ethic

Economic stability

FAILURE OF CHARTISM

No general middle-class support for cross-class alliance

Power of state (army and judiciary) enables mass arrests

Hostility of government and House of Commons

Exhaustion of constitutional means to reform

Rejection by propertied class of natural right to suffrage

Charter abandoned by majority after 1848

Chronological Table

1776   Declaration of American Independence.
Thomas Cartwright's *Take Your Choice* published.

1791   Thomas Paine's *Rights of Man* published.

1816   Hampden Clubs founded to campaign for universal suffrage.

1819   16 August, 'Peterloo Massacre' when Manchester yeomanry sent into mass meeting to arrest Henry 'Orator' Hunt - the most famous radical speaker of his day - 11 people killed.

1829   Catholic emancipation achieved by Daniel O'Connell's electoral victory in County Clare - Catholics could now become MPs.

1830-32 Reform Bill crisis.

1832   'Days of May': Confrontation between Whig government and Political Unions.
Attwood's Birmingham Political Union threatens the use of force.
June, Reform Bill passed. £10 householders enfranchised - seen by Russell and the Whigs as the final reform.
Feargus O'Connor enters Parliament as Irish MP (loses seat in 1835).

1833   Factory Act restricts child labour - significant innovation: appointment of four factory inspectors by central government.

1834   Poor Law Amendment Act signals end of Elizabethan Poor Law administered by JPs. New system centrally controlled with parishes grouped to build new workhouses, the hated 'Bastilles'.

1835   O'Connor campaigns in North - fails to win Oldham seat.

1836   London Working Men's Association (LWMA) founded. William Lovett becomes secretary.

1837   Developing campaign in northern industrial areas against new Poor Law.
Factory Movement agitating for improvement in conditions in factories and for limitation of working hours.
23 May, Attwood revives Birmingham Political Union (BPU).
7 June, LWMA sets out Six Points.
18 November, *Northern Star* first published.
Economy begins to move into a recession

1838   April, Great Northern Union (GNU) formed. O'Connor emerging as leader in North.
8 May, People's Charter published.
14 May, Birmingham takes the lead; adopts National Petition as tactic to secure the Charter.
21 May, mass meeting in Glasgow accepts Charter and Petition.

6 May, mass meeting in Birmingham marks beginning of Chartism. Attwood for BPU, O'Connor for GNU, and Henry Vincent for LWMA, share platform.

Autumn, mass meetings in textile districts lead to collection of signatures and election of delegates to proposed Convention.

27 December, government arrest J.R. Stephens - his speeches seen as incitement to riot.

1839   4 Feb, People's Parliament (the Convention) meets in London - Lovett appointed secretary.

Discussion of 'ulterior measures' alarms some delegates (particularly those from BPU) who then leave Convention.

13 May, when faced by the threat of a Tory government, likely to be more repressive than the Whigs, the Convention moves to Birmingham.

4 July, Bull Ring riots - arrest of Lovett and other Chartists.

12 July, House of Commons rejects first Petition, with 1,280,000 signatures, by 235 to 46.

August, Lovett sentenced to 12 months imprisonment.

4 November, Newport Rising - 24 Chartists killed.

1840   16 January, Frost and two others sentenced to death for high treason - later commuted to transportation for life.

February, Bronterre O'Brien sentenced to 18 months.

March, O'Connor sentenced to 18 months. 543 Chartists in prison.

20 July, National Charter Association (NCA) formed.

24 July, William Lovett released.

1841   April, Lovett founds National Association - the 'New Move'.

30 August, O'Connor released.

September, a new petitioning campaign begins.

1842   Economy moves into depression.

Mines Act ends underground labour for women and children.

Anti-Corn Law League gathers support - powerful rival to Chartists.

Leaguers and Chartists break up each others' meetings.

5 April, Joseph Sturge's Complete Suffrage Union (CSU), holds conference in Birmingham.

CSU submits its own Petition to the House of Commons - rejected by 226 to 67.

NCA presents second Petition to House of Commons with 3.3 million signatures - rejected by 287 to 49.

August, 'Plug Plot' in textile districts over pay develops into general strike when, on 12 August, Manchester Trades Conference resolves to continue strike until the Charter becomes law.

Tory Home Secretary, Sir John Graham, orders arrest of delegates, as well as O'Connor.

19 August, Miners' strike in Potteries develops into a riot.

20 August, Manchester trade societies call for a return to work.

October, trials of Staffordshire rioters - 56 transported and 116 sent to prison.

27 December, Conference of CSU and Chartists fail to reach agreement.

1843   March, Lancaster trials of those arrested in Manchester - light sentences, later quashed on technicality.

September, NCA discusses O'Connor's new Land Plan.

October, Julian Harney becomes editor of *Northern Star*.

November, *Star* moves to London from Leeds.

1845   December, NCA agrees to the Land Plan.

1846   Repeal of the Corn Laws.

1847   1 May, O'Connorville opened.

July, O'Connor becomes MP for Nottingham.

Ten Hour Factory Act. Poor Law Commission abolished.

1848   Downturn in the economy.

February, Revolution in Paris: Republic proclaimed.

4 April, Convention assembles in London.

10 April, Kennington Common mass meeting, planned to go in procession to Commons with third Petition, prohibited by Whig government, and dispersed peacefully by O'Connor. London in state of siege.

13 April, Commons contemptuously rejected Petition after House informed of the many bogus signatures on Petition

1 May, National Assembly replaces Convention.

18 May, Bradford riots.

6 June, Arrest of Ernest Jones.

July, Irish rising - prevented by arrest of leaders.

15 August, aborted London rising.

Public Health Act passed.

1850   O'Connor withdraws from leadership.

10 July, Ernest Jones released.

1851   31 March, NCA accepts social democratic programme. Jones now leader.

Land Company wound up.

1852   O'Connor becomes insane.

Northern Star closes.

1855   Death of O'Connor.

1858   Chartist Conference decides to work with radicals for limited reform.

Further Reading

There are several recent articles discussing some of the more controversial aspects of the Chartist movement which you may wish to read. In *History Sixth* (No. 1, October 1987), John Belchem's article 'The Politics of Chartism' sets the movement firmly within an established radical tradition. Edward Royle in *History Review* (No. 13, September 1992), surveys its history in 'The Origins and Nature of Chartism'. In *History Today* (Vol. 41, May 1991), Gareth Steadman Jones's article on 'The Changing Face of Nineteenth-century Britain' returns to the question of the language of Chartism, while in the issue of February 1992, Dorothy Thompson responds in 'Nineteenth-century Hidden Agendas', which considers the impact of revisionism such as that of Gareth Steadman Jones on concepts like 'class'. Hugh Cunningham in *Modern History Review* (No. 4, April 1990) surveys 'The Nature of Chartism'.

A good short interpretative assessment is J.R. Dinwiddy's *Chartism* (Historical Association, 1987) which indicates the extent of the historical debate. John Charlton's sympathetic account of the movement, written from a socialist viewpoint, *The Chartists* (Pluto Press, 1987) also has in Appendix 2 an analysis of the changes in the interpretation of Chartism by historians.

An analysis of different aspects of the movement may be found in Dorothy Thompson's *The Chartists* (Temple Smith, 1984), wise and generous in its appraisal and with a pioneering chapter on the place of women in Chartism. Edward Royle's *Chartism* (third edition, Longman, 1996), combines narrative and analysis and is full of insights. It provides a useful short collection of documents. There's a fuller collection of documents in Joe Finn's *Chartists and Chartism* (Hodder and Stoughton, 1992).

Of Chartist biographies, G.D.H. Cole's *Chartist Portraits* (Macmillan, 1965), provides short biographies of all its main leaders. J. Epstein's biography of O'Connor, *The Lion of Freedom: Feargus O'Connor, Irishman and Chartist* (Croom Helm, 1982), is invaluable not only for its portrait of Feargus O'Connor but for the wealth of material on Chartism as a whole, in particular the Conventions and the National Charter Association. J. Wiener's short biography of the architect of the Six Points, *William Lovett* (Manchester University Press, 1989), is a sympathetic appraisal of his work. Harney has been fully treated in A.R. Schoyen's *The Chartist Challenge: A Portrait of George Julian Harney* (Croom Helm, 1982), which covers not only his contribution to Chartism but also offers an analysis of his thought and his relationship with continental socialism.

There has been a wealth of local studies since Asa Briggs published *Chartist Studies* (Macmillan, 1959). Of the many, particularly useful are D. Goodway's *London Chartism 1838-1848*, for its detailed examination of the movement in the capital and two essays by Clive Behagg. The first is on the 'Birmingham Political Union' in *The Chartist Experience* edited by J. Epstein and D. Thompson. The other is on 'Birmingham Chartism', Chapter 5 of his *Politics and Production in the Early Nineteenth Century* (Routledge, 1990).

In any assessment of the failure of the Chartists, what must be taken into account is the strength of the forces ranged against them. F.C. Mather's essay 'The Government and the Chartists' in Asa Briggs's *Chartist Studies*, opens up the discussion on this important topic and J. Saville's *1848. The British State and the Chartists* (Cambridge University Press, 1987) examines in detail all aspects of this question.

The Newport Rising has been explained in many ways, as inspired by foreign agents or as the Welsh wing of a general insurrection. D.J.V. Jones in *The Last Rising. The Newport Insurrection of 1839* (Clarendon Press, 1985) sets the Rising clearly in its Welsh context and examines the social and economic tensions which triggered off the march on Newport.

Index